**materials for effective staff**

# COLLECTIVE MANAGEMENT : TEAMWORK

**Geoff Hannan**

# SIMON & SCHUSTER
# EDUCATION

# Introduction

*Collective Management: Teamwork* is designed for all those working, at whatever level, in the professional development of school managers. Heads, Deputies, Senior Teachers, Staff Development Co-ordinators and Advisors will find it of specific use in their own training and in the training of middle managers. Others will find many ideas and concepts pertinent to their own work as facilitators: be it within their own departmental teams or in the classroom.

This is not a textbook on management. Rather, it is a handbook to facilitate the learning of some *practical* management skills. All the activities are active, experiential and – importantly – challenging and fun to be involved in. I have developed them over ten years working as a freelance facilitator with adults and young people.

Theory is presented, but it is intended more as a starting-point for positive action than material for intellectual consideration. Throughout, emphasis is on the 'holistic' side of working together – an essential aspect of good management in schools. The Key Skills section at the end of the book provides a 'hands on' guide to positive people-management which will be of use to all teachers.

Good management, in common with good teaching, is about doing the 'simple things' well: creating an environment of mutual trust and respect; seeking understanding of others; being sensitive to their needs as well as your own. It is about working together with high expectations for the best possible outcomes.

## Layout and content

The *Matrix* on pages iv-v presents the title and contents of each activity and indicates its use with different groupings and possible classroom application. Notes on *Facilitating active training sessions* follow on pages vi–viii.

### Section one: Working on basics

The exercises in this section cover some basic skills I believe to be essential to the positive management of people (especially in schools):
- seeking to meet the needs of staff
- developing appropriate management styles for individual needs
- knowing and communicating one's own needs as a manager
- giving praise and recognition
- listening... *really* listening to others!
- risk-taking and being assertive

### Section two: Working together in teams

In this section I look at some 'specifics' of effective people management in schools:
- the management of change
- time management
- delegation
- leadership and teamwork skills
- negotiation
- assessing management 'performance'
- managing conflict

## Section three: Working together in appraisal

A simplistic and potentially damaging view of teacher assessment is that it is about me, the manager, telling you, the subordinate, where your shortcomings lie. More constructive is a view of appraisal as a reciprocal sharing of support: I, the manager, facilitate *your own* exploration of your developmental needs and contract my support in satisfying these needs. In this view, we are all managers of ourselves, our pupils, our colleagues and our 'bosses'. The exercises in this section are designed as the first training steps to inculcate such a system into the culture of your school:

- developing ownership and developmental planning (in general)
- creating a *positive* appraisal system
- running classroom observations


## Section four: Working on the curriculum

This section provides some exercises as starting points for managers and their teams to evaluate and develop the curriculum they manage:

- defining and sharing pedagogies
- evaluating departmental practice
- exploring the potential of cross-curricular links and projects

The *Key skills sheets* on pages 102–22 are designed for workshop participants to take away with them as a guide to good practice.

Finally, the *Resources* section includes a short Bibliography and a list of Useful Contacts.

# Matrix of Contents

| ACTIVITY NO | PAGE NO | TITLE | THEME | WHOLE GROUP | SOLO WORK | PAIR WORK | SMALL GROUP WORK | APPLICATION IN THE CLASSROOM |
|---|---|---|---|---|---|---|---|---|
| | | | **Section One: Working On Basics** | | | | | |
| 1 | 2 | The Maslow Triangle | Employees' basic needs | ✓ | | ✓ | | ✓ |
| 2 | 6 | Hippo Typing | Satisfying individual needs | ✓ | | | ✓ | ✓ |
| 3 | 12 | My Needs | Examining own professional needs | | | | ✓ | |
| 4 | 13 | Management Styles | Developmental needs | | | | ✓ | |
| 5 | 16 | Praisings | Giving praise | | | | ✓ | ✓ |
| 6 | 18 | Listen to Me! | Listening skills | | | | ✓ | ✓ |
| 7,8,9 | 21 | General Skills | Widely adaptable | | | | ✓ | ✓ |
| 10 | 22 | Risk It! | Risk taking | | | | ✓ | ✓ |
| 11 | 26 | Assert Yourself | Assertiveness | ✓ | ✓ | ✓ | | ✓ |
| | | | **Section Two: Working In Teams** | | | | | |
| 12 | 30 | The Ladder Game | Management of change | | | | ✓ | |
| 13 | 33 | 20/80 | Time management | ✓ | ✓ | | | |
| 14 | 35 | Bin It! | Delegation | | | ✓ | ✓ | ✓ |
| 15 | 38 | Patterns | Teamwork | | | | ✓ | ✓ |
| 16 | 42 | Thought Experiment | Leadership/teamwork | | | | ✓ | |
| 17 | 46 | It's Your Funeral | Leadership/personal mission | ✓ | ✓ | | | |
| 18 | 47 | Tammy Tiller's Testimonial | Leadership | ✓ | | ✓ | | |
| 19 | 48 | What's Your Role? | Leadership | | | | ✓ | ✓ |
| 20 | 53 | What's Missing? | Team development | | | | ✓ | |
| 21 | 55 | Red Cards | Negotiation | | | | ✓ | ✓ |
| 22 | 59 | 2,4,6 | Argument skills | ✓ | | | ✓ | |
| 23 | 60 | Car Park | Arbitration | | | ✓ | ✓ | ✓ |
| 24 | 61 | 20 Questions | Performance indicators | ✓ | ✓ | | | |
| 25 | 66 | Trouble-Shooting | Managing conflict | | | | ✓ | |
| | | | **Section Three: Working together in appraisal** | | | | | |
| 26 | 69 | Structured Brainstorm | Developing ownership | | | | ✓ | ✓ |
| 27 | 71 | Pros, Cons & Interesting Points Analysis | Constructing an appraisal system | | | | ✓ | ✓ |
| 28 | 74 | Oscars | Classroom observations | | ✓ | | ✓ | ✓ |
| 29 | 77 | Action Planning planning | Setting up appraisal and action | | ✓ | | | |
| 30 | 80 | Setting Up Role Plays | Appraisal training | | | | ✓ | ✓ |
| 31 | 84 | Sensitive Handling | Appraisal training | | | | ✓ | ✓ |
| 32 | 87 | Supporting | Appraisal training (reaching consensus) | | | | ✓ | ✓ |
| | | | **Section Four: Working on the curriculum** | | | | | |
| 33 | 91 | Picture Gallery | Sharing perspectives/learning | | | | ✓ | ✓ |
| 34 | 94 | Helicopter! | Cross-curricular links | ✓ | | ✓ | | |
| 35 | 96 | Centering | Cross-curricular projects | ✓ | ✓ | | | |
| 36 | 97 | Assessments | Departmental developmental needs | ✓ | ✓ | | | ✓ |
| 37–38 | 100 | The 3'E's and Hierarchies | Managing the curriculum | | ✓ | | ✓ | |

# THE KEY SKILLS SHEETS

# Resources

## Suggested reading

Blanchard, K. *The One-Minute Manager* series, Fontana/Collins.
Covey, S.R. *How to succeed with people*, Simon and Schuster, 1971.
Hunt, J.H. *Managing people at work*, Pan Books Ltd, 1981.
Maddox, R.B. *Successful negotiation*, Kogan Page Ltd, 1988.
Oakland, J.S. *Total Quality Management*, Heinemann, 1989.
Stubbs, D.R. *Assertiveness at work*, Pan Books Ltd, 1986.

## Useful contacts

Geoff Hannan
Human Resources Development,
Bank Cottage, Bourton Road,
Much Wenlock, Shropshire TF13 6AJ

The Industrial Society
Peter Runge House,
3 Carlton House Terrace,
London SW1Y 5DG

Manchester Business School
Booth Street West,
Manchester M15 6PB

# Facilitating active training sessions

I enclose below some notes (some fairly obvious, others less so) to help you make your sessions enjoyable and successful.

## Preparation

### 1 Timing
Select the most suitable day and time for your Inset if at all possible. Avoid Friday evenings, the end of half-terms and, if attendance is optional, times when other events are taking place.
Plan as far ahead as possible.
Pre-plan a follow-up or review date and time for discussion of the actions to be taken.

### 2 Place
Select a suitable venue. Neutral territory is always preferable to places with established patterns of behaviour. Staffrooms should be avoided for this reason. If your budget runs to it, outside venues (hotels etc) are ideal and help to make the session a social event as well. Choose your space for its size (adequate but not too big for active work) and its environs.

*Prepare it in advance...*

- Lay out chairs. I suggest you do *not* use a circle at the start, but a forum layout with a chair for yourself separate and facing the participants. This aids the establishment of your 'control' at the start of the session.

- Have a flip-chart and pens ready at the start (much better than a board). Position it centrally. Write on the first sheet 'Welcome to our Inset on.... '!

- Make sure the room is adequately heated and ventilated.

- Have everything you need laid out on a table (photocopied sheets etc ready to give out). This conveys the message that you know what you are doing!

- If you are going to use a video player, overhead projector etc, practise beforehand and make sure all can see the screen and hear the sound. Cue video tapes prior to showing them (so we don't get 20 minutes of Cagney and Lacey before that excellent programme on time management!) Extracts from videos should be chosen for their brevity. You can legally record and reshow all TV programmes with the (E) mark.

### 3 Agendas
Well before the date of the session give each participant a sheet outlining the Inset. Post it, as well, on the Staffroom notice board. Define objectives and the timings of the session on this sheet. Use the words 'promptly please' by the starting time and make it ten minutes before you need to start!
  If possible, remind each participant personally a couple of days before the session.
  It is useful, in involvement and ownership terms, to ask people to bring along with them something relevant to the training theme. If your session is about management problems, for example, ask them to bring along an analysis in note form of a recent difficulty. Finally on the sheet state that the session is designed to lead to action.

### 4 Arrival
Be there first! Greet people at the door and thank them for coming. Give them another copy of the agenda!
  Provide refreshments at the start of the session and allow time (but not too much time) for them, especially if it's an after-school session.

A display of materials, books etc is very useful in setting the scene and conveys the fact that you've done your homework and know your stuff!

## 5 Starting off

Prepare and practise out loud (in front of a mirror even!) a very brief introduction. Thank people for coming and reiterate the objectives of the Inset. Explain that the session is totally practical but reassure them... *You are not going to be asked to play trees or do anything that puts teachers off this kind of activity! Get going.*

## 6 Issuing instructions

Prepare and practise these in advance. You may find the following guidelines useful:

- Be assertive. Avoid phrasing instructions in the *Could we perhaps move the chairs to the side please?* mode.

- Anticipate compliance by using 'Thank you', eg *Would you move the chairs back and stand in the centre...Thank you!*

- Reinforce the Thank You after the activity...*Thanks a lot. The first exercise is...*

- Always explain the point of each exercise or state that you will be debriefing it afterwards. The latter is the preferred method for much of the material in this book. Find ways of telling the participants that they will enjoy the activity (as it helps them to do so!). For example, *As well as enjoying the activities you'll find they have a lot of practical relevance for your work. OR As well as being great fun, they are also rich in content.* Again, avoid *I think you'll enjoy this exercise....* they *will* enjoy it.

- Stop an activity or call the group together by another Thank you. Never worry about repeating it... *Thank you... Thank you!*

## 7 Handling discussion

Here are some hints to help you not to get bogged down or side-tracked and to sustain a positive atmosphere...

- Open discussion by asking what people 'feel', not what they 'think'. People who say what they feel tend to produce a more considered and less immediately critical response.

- Thank each person for their contribution. Used occasionally the 'mirroring' device can be most effective in generating positivity and further contributions. The formula is as follows: *Yes, thank you for that... so you feel...* (Here you paraphrase briefly what the contributor has said.) *What do other people feel about it?*

- Keep chairpersonship of the discussion by the above formula. Never allow more than two consecutive contributions without you 'getting in'. This is especially important if the discussion is getting argumentative...
  *Thank you, Janet and Graham... anyone else like to add anything?*

- Avoid making statements yourself if possible. It's far better to get the participants to make your points for you. Here is a useful tool in difficult moments such as responding to provocation... *Yes... Thank you, Martin... would anyone like to answer that point? No, Martin, I'm not avoiding it... I shall tell you what I feel in a minute.*

- Conclude discussion by thanking the contributors and stating that it has been interesting and useful. *Let's move on now...*

## 8 Handling debrief

All of the above plus... Prior to the session list the points you want to bring out and lead the participants through them sequentially. If you use your flipchart to note the points raised by individuals, write down *verbatim* what is said, using their words or a paraphrase with their approval... *If I put down xxxxx does this cover your point?* At the end, sum up the points the participants have made.

## 9 Length of activities

I have stated approximate timings, but gauge them yourself. The golden rule is 'Leave them wanting more'. Don't let the exercises drag on just so all the points are covered. On stopping an exercise the best response you can get is 'we need a bit longer!' (so give them it). If one group finishes before the others, go over to them and tell them you'll be stopping the activity soon. Ask them for their feelings about the exercise. If you have six groups and the exercise is going well, wait for the third group to finish and then stop the activity. The handouts at the back of the book may be useful to give to the early finishers.

## 10 Targetting

It is important that each training session produces something tangible, a commitment by the participants to take action or a feeling that further attention to the issues is needed. Where time allows, hold a brief plenary where each participant or department states what action they intend to take. Minute these and let everyone have a copy afterwards. Ask them to report back during the review session.

## 11 Concluding

Finish earlier than stated! Sum up briefly what has been achieved. *Thank you for coming. I hope you have found the session enjoyable and useful!*

Have fun!

# Section One: Working on basics

I would love to be
a puppeteer
dancing you to the sounds
of happy children
but I think I feel
from above
strings

# Activity 1 The Maslow Triangle

The American psychologist Abraham H. Maslow described a 'hierarchy of needs' common to all people, in the form of a pyramid (as shown on Sheet 1.2). This is a very useful starting point for getting managers to ask themselves a basic question: are we satisfying the needs of our staff? The way the following session works also illustrates a couple of devices for you the trainer to use to add a little bit of 'magic' to a workshop.

## Objectives

To draw attention to the manager's role in creating a caring relationship with staff
To highlight some positive approaches for so doing

## Target group

All management levels

*Pair work* from whole group, then back to whole group

## Duration

About an hour

## Materials

One copy of Sheet 1.1 *Life and all that*
Masking tape
A set of five cards (say 30 cm × 15 cm) each with one of the following headings: (1) SURVIVAL (2) SECURITY    (3) BELONGING
(4) PRESTIGE    (5) SELF-ACTUALISATION
One copy of Sheet 1.2 *Key questions* for each participant to take away with them
Pens and paper

## Operation

1  Before the start of the session prepare the room. Move chairs to the side. In the centre of the floor map out the triangle using masking tape. Divide the triangle as follows:

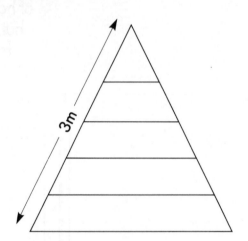

This provides a focal point as people arrive at the workshop... something a little different to spark-off interest can have quite a significant effect upon the participants' involvement in the session. Don't explain what it's about, they'll discover it! Also, as you will see later, it provides you with a highly effective way of sharing ideas.

2  (The start of the session.) Ask the group to sit around the triangle and invite them to listen to a short story. Read them the story on Sheet 1.1.

This is the second training device – using two stimuli concurrently. The group listen to a humorous introduction. (This is useful in itself to introduce serious ideas as it 'humanises' what might otherwise have been received as a cold piece of theory.) As they look at the plan on the floor, they will be trying to equate what they hear to what they see. This, I believe, helps to provoke a creative response which they will use to good effect later when they relate the theory to their own values and experiences.

3 After reading the story, go to the triangle and use the heading cards to label the sections. From the base, the labels will be SURVIVAL, SECURITY, BELONGING, PRESTIGE, SELF-ACTUALISATION. Explain briefly that the triangle or pyramid represents a hierarchy of needs presented by Maslow.

4 Divide the group into pairs. Give each pair a sheet of A4 paper and set the following task:

*You are HMIs visiting a school. You are using the Maslow hierarchy of needs as criteria for assessing the quality of management within this school. Select one of the headings and devise two searching questions you would ask a HoD to find out whether or not they are helping to satisfy the professional needs of their staff. For example, a HoD would have responsibility for aiding a colleague's 'survival' in the classroom, so you might ask them 'What support do you provide for members of the team who find class control to be a problem?'*

This is a difficult exercise, aided, I feel, by the visualisation process you have previously taken them through. Allow 20 minutes or so for it, and give assistance where needed.

5 Stop the activity. Ask the pairs to lay their questions out under the appropriate headings on the central triangle. Invite them to go around the triangle and read what the other pairs have written (a neat way of sharing ideas).

6 *Action task* Give each person another piece of paper. Ask them to note down three or four new things they could do as managers to help satisfy the needs of their own teams. Get them to do this on their own. (Remind them that there are some ideas on the floor in front of them!)
(*Ten to 15 minutes*)

7 Reassemble the group to share ideas. Conclude by giving each participant a copy of Sheet 1.2 *Key questions* for further consideration.

## In the classroom...

You could use the triangle as a focus during tutor group work to get the class to define their needs within school; applying a similar whole and pair work format. You may well find that 'survival' and 'security' open up discussion on issues such as bullying. Pupils could, for example, list problems they have under the headings.

## Key skills sheet 5

# Life and all that

What appeared to be Adam's eyes opened.

'Hello,' he thought, 'who am I? Or, for that matter, where am I? Or, even more to the point, whoever I am and wherever I am; how the hell did I get here?'

Adam pursued this somewhat cyclical line of self-enquiry for a full 30 seconds before realising its futility and with great difficulty discovered 'standing up'.

'Now they're natty!' he thought to himself, discovering his legs. 'And wow, look at these!' he rejoiced, swinging his arms about. 'And each one of these digital appendices stuck on the end of them moves, that might prove useful!'

Adam bounced around for several hours in sheer delight (before discovering that placing one foot in front of the other produced a more comfortable method of propulsion).

Suddenly a thought struck him. Words began to form on his lips: 'I nnnn... eeeed... I need... I need! I need?'

Adam noticed that on what appeared to be a tree was hanging what appeared to be a bunch of slim bent yellow objects.

He further noticed that raising his arm in their direction and making use of the potentially useful digital appendices resulted in not just one but 347 of the aforementioned objects falling down on top of him. He called this discovery 'Irony'.

Noticing one of the slim bent yellow objects on the ground he was suddenly overcome by an inexplicable desire to stuff it into his body.

'Ah, this must be an intuitive biochemical drive!' he guessed. 'But how does one satisfy it?'

'Logic would seem to suggest that in order to get this slim bent yellow object into my body, there must be a point of access: an orifice designed specifically for that purpose. I shall explore the possibilities.'

Adam explored the possibilities.

Eventually he discovered his mouth and stuck the banana in it. 'Oh joy', he thought, 'I have discovered my first need. I need to 'Survive'!'

Adam spent many happy hours satisfying his need to survive before discovering that just surviving seemed a pretty damn boring way of spending his time.

'I shall go forth and find myself some more needs!' He short-term targetted.

It started to rain.

'Oh joy, what fun, I need to build myself a shelter, I have discovered my second need, I need 'Security'!'

Adam sat in his newly-built shelter. As the rain dripped down on his head he pondered where he might discover his next need from. He felt lonely and sad. Yes, he needed to 'Belong'.

Fortunately a band of merry cave dwellers were passing doing the sort of things merry cave dwellers do when they pass you.

'I say old chap you look frightfully sad!' said the passing merry cave dwellers to Adam in passing. 'Would you like to come and live in our cave with us and do the sorts of things we merry cave dwellers do, ie our 'Corporate Culture'?'

'Super!' replied Adam, discovering new ways of speaking and jargon to speak it in.

Some months later, sitting merrily in the merry cave dwellers' cave merrily doing the sorts of things merry cave dwellers do, Adam suddenly felt cold. He began to shiver. He got out his electric fire and plugged it in.

For the first time the cave was warm. The merry cave dwellers cheered and acclaimed Adam and gave him yet another need, 'Prestige'.

'You've done a good job for us,' the merry cave dwellers told Adam. 'We have decided in return to tell you how to get your fifth and final need.'

With feet firmly on the ground, look to the mountains. Help us to survive the path upwards. Give us the security of foot-hold we need. Make us feel part of your mission. Praise us when we do a good job. And find for yourself, through us, the satisfaction of your fifth and final need: 'Self-actualisation'.

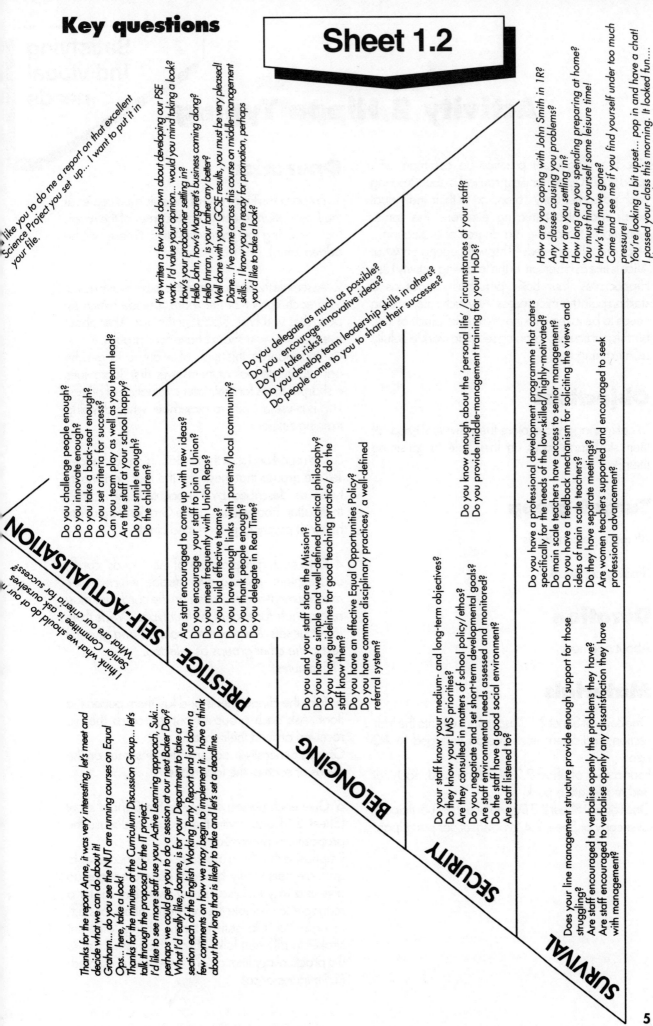

*...like you to do me a report on that excellent Science Project you set up... I want to put it in your file.*

*I've written a few ideas down about developing our PSE work. I'd value your opinion... would you mind taking a look?*
*How's your probationer settling in?*
*Hello John, how's Margaret's business coming along?*
*Hello Imran, is your father any better?*
*Well done with your GCSE results, you must be very pleased!*
*Diane... I've come across this course on middle-management skills... I know you're ready for promotion, perhaps you'd like to take a look?*

*How are you coping with John Smith in 1R?*
*Any classes causing you problems?*
*How are you settling in?*
*How long are you spending preparing at home?*
*You must find yourself some leisure time!*
*How's the move gone?*
*Come and see me if you find yourself under too much pressure!*
*You're looking a bit upset... pop in and have a chat!*
*I passed your class this morning. It looked fun.... what were you doing?*

## SELF-ACTUALISATION

Do you challenge people enough?
Do you innovate enough?
Do you take a back-seat enough?
Do you set criteria for success?
Can you team play as well as you team lead?
Are the staff at your school happy?
Do you smile enough?
Do the children?

Do you delegate as much as possible?
Do you encourage innovative ideas?
Do you take risks?
Do you develop team leadership skills in others?
Do people come to you to share their successes?

## PRESTIGE

Are staff encouraged to come up with new ideas?
Do you encourage your staff to join a Union?
Do you meet frequently with Union Reps?
Do you build effective teams?
Do you have enough links with parents/local community?
Do you thank people enough?
Do you delegate in Real Time?

Do you know enough about the 'personal life'/circumstances of your staff?
Do you provide middle-management training for your HoDs?

Do you and your staff share the Mission?
Do you have a simple and well-defined practical philosophy?
Do you have guidelines for good teaching practice/ do the staff know them?
Do you have an effective Equal Opportunities Policy?
Do you have common disciplinary practices/ a well-defined referral system?

Do you have a professional development programme that caters specifically for the needs of the low-skilled/highly-motivated?
Do main scale teachers have access to senior management?
Do you have a feedback mechanism for soliciting the views and ideas of main scale teachers?
Do they have separate meetings?
Are women teachers supported and encouraged to seek professional advancement?

## BELONGING

*Thanks for the report Anne, it was very interesting, let's meet and decide what we can do about it!*
*Graham... do you see the NUT are running courses on Equal Ops... here, take a look!*
*Thanks for the minutes of the Curriculum Discussion Group... let's talk through the proposal for the IT project.*
*I'd like to see more staff use your Active Learning approach, Suki... perhaps we could get you to do a session at our next Baker Day?*
*What I'd really like, Joanne, is for your Department to take a section each of the English Working Party Report and jot down a few comments on how we may begin to implement it... have a think about how long that is likely to take and let's set a deadline.*

## SECURITY

Do your staff know your medium- and long-term objectives?
Do they know your LMS priorities?
Are they consulted in matters of school policy/ethos?
Do you negotiate and set short-term developmental goals?
Are staff environmental needs assessed and monitored?
Do the staff have a good social environment?
Are staff listened to?

## SURVIVAL

Does your line management structure provide enough support for those struggling?
Are staff encouraged to verbalise openly the problems they have?
Are staff encouraged to verbalise openly any dissatisfaction they have with management?

*I think what we should do at our next Senior Committee is ask ourselves... What are our criteria for success?*

5

# Activity 2 Hippo Typing

Good management practice (in common with good Equal Opportunities practice) is about treating each person equally according to their individual needs, not about treating everyone the same. Involved in the above is a degree of evaluation... what are Alice's needs? This will depend on what Alice is like as a person. In the following activity I use Hippocrates' four basic personality types as a starting point for this process. Any such categorising needs to be taken with the proverbial pinch of salt, but this particular seasoning seems to work tastefully as a training tool...

## Objectives

To get managers to explore the individual needs of their staff (and focus on their role in satisfying them!)

## Target group

All management levels

*Small group work*

## Duration

About one hour

## Materials

One copy of Sheet 2.1 *Descriptions* cut into the four sections indicated; each section enlarged to A3 size
Four copies of Sheet 2.2 *Needs* on card, each cut and made into a pack
One copy of Sheet 2.3 *Debrief sheet* per participant
One copy of Sheet 2.4 *Worksheet* per participant

## Operation

1 *Preparation* Place one of the enlarged copies of the *Descriptions* sheet, in each corner of the room, first removing the character titles. (These will be added later.)

2 Assemble the participants and explain as follows: *Visit each corner of the room. Decide which list describes you best. Stand by that list.* After about five minutes, you should have four groups.
It's important in this type of exercise to get the participants to look at themselves first. It provides a sharper focus for their later evaluation of others. This is a useful point to remember when devising training sessions.

3 Go round and stick the title labels on each sheet. Tell the groups that these are the four personality types as described by Hippocrates (he named them after 'bodily fluids'... the Greeks were a little better at psychology than medicine!)

4 Give each group a pack of the 'Needs' cards, and explain: *As a group, decide which of the management needs written on the cards are most appropriate for each of the four types. Divide them into four sets. Keep one for yourself and give the rest to the other groups as selected.*
*(15 minutes)*

5 Take the Hippo sheets and lay them out on the floor. Ask each group to put the cards they've received around their sheet.
Groups generally reach a wide consensus on the needs of each of the four types.

6 Give each person a copy of the *Debrief sheet* (Sheet 2.3) and invite the group to discuss the propositions presented.
Emphasise that there are no accurate measures to evaluate personality but such generalisations do give us a way-in. Discuss how important it is for a manager to evaluate the individual needs of staff, in order to help satisfy them, giving 'different strokes to different folks'. Elicit their responses to the practical application of the theories presented.
*(15 minutes or so)*

7  *Action task* Give each participant a copy of the *Worksheet* (Sheet 2.4) and ask them to complete it as instructed.
*(20 minutes)*

8  Bring everyone together to share their questions, reservations, difficulties etc. Ask them to put the action plan to work!

## In the classroom...

You could devise other lists of words for young people to make decisions about themselves (eg descriptions of behaviour in school). This provides a strong focus for them to examine their attitudes, etc. I've run the Hippo exercise with Year 11 pupils with words and phrases evaluating assertive qualities (see Activity 11 *Assert Yourself*) – getting them first to be honest about how they are in situations and then to explore how they would like to be.

Key skills sheets 1 and 5 >

## Descriptions

### Choleric... the innovator

Thruster

Achiever

Lots of ideas person

Charismatic

Over-the-top at times

Solver of problems

Strong

Autocratic

A bad team player

### Phlegmatic... the cautious

Consistent

Sensitive

Careful

Efficient

A plodder

Reliable

Co-operative

### Sanguine... the manipulator

Adaptable

Dynamic

Wanting to please

Diplomatic

A mind changer

Sophisticated

Flexible

Democratic

A good team player

### Melancholic... the systems' person

Systematic

Hyper-efficient

Bureaucratic

Supportive

Precise

Punctual

Tidy

Shy

Self-effacing

## Needs

| Lots of different challenges | Told carefully *what* you want | Appreciation of abilities |
|---|---|---|
| Training in new skills | Course correction | Excitement and short-term goals |
| Public appreciation | A consistent managerial approach | Working with different people |
| Medium-term goals | Variety in their work | Consultative guidance |
| Stability | Told *how* to do things | Time to adapt to change |
| Bringing out of real feelings | Long-term goals with careful reviewing | Sensitive handling |
| Harmony | Long-term goals fully negotiated | Delegation |
| Show *why* something needs to be done | Avoid criticism | Praise privately |

## Debrief Sheet

There is, of course, a great danger in labelling! Each individual is different and has different needs. The following is designed as a generalised 'tool' to assist as a starting point for assessing the needs of specific individuals.

| 'TYPE' | WHAT THEY ARE MOST LIKELY TO NEED FROM YOU |
|---|---|
| **Choleric – the innovator** | |
| thruster | Short-term goals |
| achiever | Lots of encouragement and praise |
| lots of ideas person | Public recognition of their achievements |
| charismatic | Opportunity to develop new skills and interests |
| 'over the top' at times | Sensitive monitoring and course correction |
| solver of problems | |
| strong | |
| autocratic | |
| a bad team player | |
| **Sanguine – the manipulator** | |
| adaptable | Medium-term goals |
| dynamic | Consultatory guidance |
| wanting to please | A consistent managerial approach |
| diplomatic | To be involved in lots of different things with |
| a mind changer | different people |
| sophisticated | |
| flexible | |
| democratic | |
| a good team player | |
| **Phlegmatic – the cautious** | |
| consistent | Long-term goals, with careful and periodic |
| sensitive | reviewing |
| careful | To be told what you want |
| efficient | Sensitive handling and time to explore their real |
| a plodder | feelings |
| reliable | Lots of stability and time to adapt to change |
| co-operative | |
| **Melancholic – the systems person** | |
| systematic | Long-term goals, fully negotiated |
| hyper-efficient | Harmony |
| bureaucratic | A detailed brief with explanation of reasons |
| supportive | Plenty of delegated responsibilities |
| precise | Lots of time to do things |
| punctual | |
| tidy | |
| shy | |
| self-effacing | |

## Worksheet

1 Enter in Column 1 the names of your Department/Team.
2 For each, in Column 2, select three words that you would use to describe them.
3 In Column 3, for each word selected to describe the individual members of your department, assess the kind of managerial support these descriptions would suggest you need to provide.
4 On the Development Line, define a short-term objective you have for their professional development.
5 On the How Line, define the actions you will take as a manager to achieve the above developmental objective.

| 1 | 2 | 3 |
|---|---|---|
| **Colleague's name** | **Descriptive words** | **Support needed** |
| _____ | _____ | _____ |
| | _____ | _____ |
| | _____ | _____ |

**Development** _____
**How** _____

- - - - - - - - - - - - - - - - - - - - - - - - - - - - - - - - - - - - - - - - -

| **Colleague's name** | **Descriptive words** | **Support needed** |
|---|---|---|
| _____ | _____ | _____ |
| | _____ | _____ |
| | _____ | _____ |

**Development** _____
**How** _____

- - - - - - - - - - - - - - - - - - - - - - - - - - - - - - - - - - - - - - - - -

| **Colleague's name** | **Descriptive words** | **Support needed** |
|---|---|---|
| _____ | _____ | _____ |
| | _____ | _____ |
| | _____ | _____ |

**Development** _____
**How** _____

- - - - - - - - - - - - - - - - - - - - - - - - - - - - - - - - - - - - - - - - -

| **Colleague's name** | **Descriptive words** | **Support needed** |
|---|---|---|
| _____ | _____ | _____ |
| | _____ | _____ |
| | _____ | _____ |

**Development** _____
**How** _____

# Activity 3 My needs

Management should be a reciprocal process. As well as giving to their subordinates, a manager needs to get something back!

## Objectives

To get the participants to explore their own needs in the management relationship and discuss how they can get their team to satisfy them!

## Target group

All management levels

*Small groups* of four

## Duration

About one hour

## Materials

A pack of *Needs cards* (Sheet 2.2 from Activity 2) for each group
Pens and paper

## Operation

1 Divide participants into groups of four. Give each group a pack of *Needs cards* (Sheet 2.2). Tell them that each person is to select three of the cards as being the needs they feel they have as managers. (Better still...knowing the people you are working with, you could make up your own Needs pack.) If they all want the same card they must negotiate... saying why their need is more pressing than the others. This generates a lot of laughs, but it also opens them up to discussing the problems they feel they have with their teams.

2 Debrief some of these problems and discuss the importance of having one's own needs satisfied.

3 Invite participants to work individually to assess their own needs under three categories: short-term, medium-term and long-term. Get them to write their needs on a piece of paper.

4 Reform the groups and ask them to discuss each person's professional needs in turn, suggesting ways they might approach getting their teams to be sensitive to them.

5 A useful *action task* is to target one short-term need and action plan for its resolution.

# Activity 4 Management Styles

'Different strokes for different folks' is at the heart of good management practice. 'Different strokes for the same folks' are also needed...

## Objectives

To give a grounding in developmental theory and relate it practically to managerial approaches.

## Target group

All management levels

*Small groups* of four

## Duration

About one hour

## Materials

A pack of *Needs cards* (Sheet 2.2 from Activity 2) for each group
A copy of Sheet 4.1 *Stages* for each group
A copy of Sheet 4.2 *Management styles* for each participant
Pens and paper

## Operation

1 Divide participants into groups of four. Give each group a pack of *Needs cards* and a copy of Sheet 4.1. Explain as follows:

*Chris Brown has passed through a number of stages in her/his teaching career. These 'developmental' stages are common to many people in organisations like schools. During each of these stages a good manager will be aware of their colleague's needs and seek to satisfy them...*
  *Divide the cards under each of the headings on the sheet, according to which you think is the most appropriate managerial approach to take with a person at each stage in their development.*

Emphasise that careful consideration and discussion is the reason for this exercise; the point is not to produce a set of 'right' answers.
(*Allow about 20 minutes*)

2 Discuss their findings. Introduce the three basic management styles: Directional, Delegatory and Consultatory. Work through the *Management styles* sheet (4.2).

3 A useful *action task* is to get participants to write down the names of their teams on a piece of paper and to use the *Management styles* sheet to help construct a tight definition of the most appropriate managerial approach for each team member.

# Stages

Chris Brown looks back over a career in teaching and sees it as a passage through four stages:

### Stage One: Low skills and high motivation
Beginning career. Chris is highly motivated but with few skills....

### Stage Two: Medium skills and medium motivation
A few years in now... Chris has developed a number of skills (no longer has any problems with class control, for example) but things are getting a bit too easy and motivation seems to be dropping.

### Stage Three: High skills and low motivation
Chris has been a teacher for ten years and knows all the tricks of the trade. The kids are easy to handle now. But Chris is bored and isn't enjoying it any more!

### Stage Four: High skills and high motivation
Chris gains a new lease of life! Having a great time now! How to keep it this way?

# Management styles

## DIRECTIONAL (for Chris' first stage)

When someone is just starting out and is highly motivated the best style to use is Directional – suggesting how to do things. Don't support too much... let them make their own mistakes but be there to help them solve the problems this causes.

**Example** *This would be the appropriate style to use with a probationary teacher with lots of ideals and enthusiasm but few classroom management skills to put these into practice.*

## DELEGATORY (for Chris' second stage)

When someone is developing their skills and things become easier, it's their motivation that might need boosting. Direct less and support their motivation by delegating more to them.

**Example** *The delegatory style would suit a main scale teacher in their second/third year of teaching perhaps, who has learnt some effective approaches to classroom management and has good control and rapport with pupils. You could give them specific teaching responsibilities within the department (eg planning a specific unit of work/leading the team-teaching in certain curriculum areas).*

## CONSULTATORY AND DELEGATORY (for Chris' third and fourth stages)

When someone has a lot of skills, things might become too easy and boring for them. No direction is now needed. What is needed is a recognition of their skills through consultation and delegation of responsibilities with further skill development through new challenges. This will help maintain high motivation – or revive it if it seems to be flagging.

**Example** *Someone who has been at the school with little or no promotion for a long time would benefit from a consultatory/delegatory approach. You could engage them in planning new initiatives with you and then give them responsibility for enactment (eg initiating and running a cross-curricular project with other departments).*

# Activity 5 Praisings

We all need a pat on the back. We all need not only to feel but to be *told* that we are doing a good job. We all need praise. But how often do we get it? Our first response to anything tends to be a critical one. Perhaps it's the way we are brought up; with the idea that we could all do that bit better? Our very best efforts met with an A minus! A prime task of management is to make people feel good about themselves; to make them feel secure and confident in their own abilities and actions. We are all very poor at giving praise and equally bad at receiving it. This activity is a must for anyone involved in training! Use it and a number of things will strike you. First, how starved of praise people are (as the sheer involvement in the activity will show you – stop it before everyone has had a go at your peril!) Second, how difficult people find it to take praise. And third, how few managers have ever really thought about the significance of praising staff. Use it as a warm-up to any other activity, or with the action task below as an important session on its own...

## Objectives

To explore the importance of praise-orientated management
To target the above as a specific development in the participants' management styles

## Target groups

All levels

*Small groups* of four

## Duration

One hour

## Materials

Pens and paper

## Operation

1 Assemble the participants in groups in circles.

2 Ask them *in turn* around the circle to list single words that have a connotation that is positive; for example words they might use to compliment another person.
Ask them to keep going around the group until you stop the activity.
(*About five minutes*)

3 Ask the groups to rearrange themselves into a semi-circle. Give each group another chair, placing it facing their semi-circle.

4 Explain the task....
*Each person in turn sits in the chair facing the others. In turn the others make a statement about this person. The statement must be entirely positive. You have to say what you like about them! No joking is allowed.*
*The person seated alone may not reply. Go around the group at least twice. Each statement must be different.*
This takes about 15 minutes and you won't be allowed to stop it until everyone has had a go at being praised!

5 Debrief the following....
● *How difficult we find receiving praise. Why is this?*
● *Do we find it equally difficult to give praise?* Discuss the following propositions...
● *People who feel good about themselves produce good results.*
● *If we as managers show our appreciation of people consistently and openly we lay the ground for developing a strong professional relationship built upon mutual esteem.*
● *If we always find ways of being positive in our handling of others then, when reprimand or criticism is needed it is received more positively and fruitfully.*
(*20 minutes*)

*6 Action task...*
Ask each participant to list the names of their direct subordinates. Ask them to study the list and ask themselves, honestly, when was the last time they went out of their way to praise these people, individually and openly. Get them to think about ways they could do this, without it coming as a shock or seeming stilted! If necessary, add a suggestion: *One way is to say to your team 'I don't feel that I've been showing as much appreciation of your efforts as I should. From now on, I'm going to make a special effort to tell you my feelings when you're doing something well. After all, we do it to the kids, perhaps we all need more praise ourselves!'*

## In the classroom...

Try the round-circle praisings with young people. They love it but find it terribly difficult (almost as difficult as adults!) Talk about the tendency children have to put one-another down and the importance of providing support for one-another.

**Key skills sheets 4 and 5**

# Activity 6 Listen to Me!

After working one Inset day with a group of mainscale teachers and the next with a group of Heads, a curious phenomenon struck me. I played a simple warm-up game that involved listening closely to one-another. The mainscale group completed the task quickly. The Headteachers found it much more difficult! There seems to be an inverse relationship between managerial status and listening abilities! I have since observed this with other groups. It seems the more we know the less inclined we are to listen to others! The irony is, of course, that the reverse is actually true. The higher up in management we are, the more we *need* to listen! Apart from anything else, listening is a fundamental way of giving another person prestige. There are key listening skills that anybody can learn. Use the exercise below as a very effective warm-up to group work tasks, or in conjunction with Key skills sheet 1 as a 'complete' workshop on listening skills.

## Objectives

To explore the significance of effective listening
To teach key listening skills

## Target groups

All levels

*Small groups* of four

## Duration

One hour

## Materials

A copy of Sheet 6.1 *Ideas* divided into four for each group.
A copy of *Key skills sheet 1* for each participant.

## Operation

1 Divide participants into groups of four and sit them in a small circle.

2 Give each group member a different section of Sheet 6.1 and explain the task...
*In turn around the group you are going to explain the idea written on your sheet. You must explain it as if it is your idea and, hence, as if you totally agree with it. Take a few minutes to come to grips with the idea, so you will be able to communicate it more easily. You can refer to your card during the task.*
(*Allow a few minutes*)

3 Start the game with the following instruction:
*Each person in the group must explain their idea to the rest. The remainder of the group are 'the listeners'. Their task is to fully understand the difficult concept the speaker (with very little preparation) is attempting to expound. They are not allowed to make any statements themselves, but are allowed to ask questions!*
(*About 15 minutes*)

4 Debrief by introducing the following as key listening skills:
● *Looking at the person who's talking is the first important thing the listener should do.*
● *To make this eye-contact comfortable for the speaker and to build their confidence in speaking, nodding is a highly effective response (as opposed to nodding-off!).*
● *Prior to asking questions for further clarification of the speaker's ideas, paraphrase back to them what they have just said... 'So you think a, b, and c... what about d?' This is a very important key to effective listening. It shows the speaker you are listening closely (you have to be to do it); it gives them confidence and aids them in communicating more precisely.*

If you want to use the game just as a warm-up, proceed now to another group work task. It's well worth using it in this way, as the quality of the group work will be much better after this activity. To further explore listening skills themselves, proceed with the following...

5 Discuss briefly the difference between just hearing what has been said and listening with the intention of fully understanding the feelings behind what is being said.

6 Ask each group member to speak in turn about their philosophy of education! Tell them you will give them just a couple of minutes to think through what they are going to say. Give them the couple of minutes.

7 Instruct them as follows...
*The listeners' role now is to help the speaker to fully expound their theory. Do this by paraphasing first what the speaker has just said, prior to asking each question. (It will seem a little stilted at first, but you and they will notice a dramatic change in the quality of the listening. Most noticeable is the body language the listeners will now adopt: leaning into the group intently and nodding in response!)*

8 Give each participant a copy of *Key Skills Sheet 1* and discuss it.

9 *Action task* Next time they are listening to a colleague, ask them to make a point of using the repetition technique.

## In the classroom...

Listening skills are of obvious significance. I have used the 'explain and question' technique to great success with teenagers. Introducing a time element can be quite fun: *The speaker explains the subject: you have just one minute to ask as many questions as you can.*

## Key skills sheet 1

# Ideas

### Operant Learning

Operant Learning is learning through reinforcement of past behaviour. We learn not to do some things because of negative reinforcement and to do other things by positive reinforcement. The latter is a more productive method of learning.

------------------------------------------------✂

### Conditioning

This is a type of learning explored by Pavlov and his famous dogs. For conditioning to take place *two* stimuli have to be presented simultaneously or a new stimulus presented slightly *prior* to the old one. Almost no learning takes place if the old stimulus is presented first. This has ramifications for the teacher in the classroom...

------------------------------------------------✂

### Remembering

We remember what we have experienced first-hand much better than what we have been told about. Therefore, if we want children to remember the content of lessons it is best to teach it experientially.

------------------------------------------------✂

### Reasoning

Reasoning is a form of thinking where possible solutions are tested *symbolically*. Since much learning depends on reasoning and since reasoning is language-dependent; language development is an important part of all teachers' work.

# Activities 7,8,9

The following are some adaptable ideas based on listening skills but with wider applications. They are good 'starters' to get everyone focused on your theme. All three activities can be adapted for classroom use.

## Activity 7 A good manager needs...

This is based on the children's game 'I went to the shops to buy...' Start with a basic statement and go round the group. Each person adds to the list after repeating what has just been said, ie A *I went to the shop to buy carrots.* B *I went to the shop to buy carrots and peas.* C *I went to the shop to buy carrots, peas and bananas* etc. One adaptation could be to start with the statement: *A good manager needs...*
**Objectives** Developing listening skills, concentration and exploring ideas. (The less obvious skills will be contributed later in the game when the obvious ones have been used up.)

## Activity 8 Secret messages

'Secret messages' is a versatile idea for initiating discussion. A sheet of lined paper and a pen are passed around the group. The first person writes on the top line, folds it over the back of the sheet and passes it on to the second. The second person cannot read the first line but adds one of their own, folds the paper and passes it on... In this context, for example, the first person might write: *The most important skill a manager needs is leadership;* the second: *The most important skill a manager needs is delegation...* and so on.
**Objectives** Developing listening skills (all will be keen to listen to what the others have written!) and getting each participant to share their personal criteria for good management. They could, for example, examine the similarities and explore how a manager might present such qualities to their subordinates.

## Activity 9 Suggestion box

Each group gets a shoebox. Anonymously, each member writes something on a piece of paper, folds it and puts it in the box. The contents are then read out. The following adaptation would be useful for HoDs: *You've left this box in your room for members of your team to suggest ways you might improve the running of your department. Write down what you think the most common suggestion would be!*
**Objectives** Listening skills development again (because of the interest the game quickly generates) and sharing ideas on developmental possibilities.
A nice Action Task for this activity is to get the participants to put up a suggestion box for their team!

# Activity 10 Risk It!

We have a tendency to become 'risk-averse' in our management of people and systems. Our teaching styles and our management styles seem to work well, why change them? Why look for new approaches? The answer is because society changes; the needs of children change; the people we manage develop their own expertise and, thus, change in what they need from us. Change is the natural dynamic of everything 'vital'! Change, if managed well, is good for people. New initiatives can fuel new energies, build new perspectives, find new solutions to old problems.

I suggest that the ability to take risks lies at the heart of effective change management. This means daring to invest people with slightly more responsibility than we might be tempted to; to demand from ourselves and others slightly higher standards than we might dare to hope for; ... to resist being purely conservative and dare to be innovative! Here's a remarkable little game which will provoke discussion on these points...

## Objectives

To encourage risk-taking
To stimulate discussion on the advantages of risk-taking with people

## Target group

Senior and middle management

*Small groups* – a maximum of six

## Duration

One hour

## Materials

One copy each of Sheets 10.1 and 10.2 stuck on to card and cut as indicated. (Arrange the small cards thus produced into a pack, *in order*, with card number one on top.) One set per group.
Paper and pens

## Operation

1  Divide participants into groups and sit them in a small circle. Give each group a pack of cards.

2  Instruct them in playing the game...
*There are 16 cards in the pack.*
*There is a sum of money written on each card.*
*The object of the game is to secure the largest possible sum of money.*
*Place the cards in the centre of the group, face down.*
*Take turns to turn over the cards, one at a time.*
*The sum on the card is offered to people in turn, around the circle. (Each new card must be offered first to a different person in the circle.) The person offered the card may either accept or pass.*
● *if they accept, they receive that sum of (imaginary!) money. They are then out of the game.*
● *if they pass, the card is offered to the next person, and so on until someone accepts.*
● *if everyone passes, that card is out of the game and you proceed to the next card.*
*(It's much easier played than it looks... try it out on someone prior to using it in training! The results are very interesting. Usually in a group of six, by the time you get to the maximum sum of £1000 there is just one person left still in the game, who takes it: thus avoiding the final four 'nothing' cards!)*
*(The game takes about ten to 15 minutes)*

3  Bring groups together, debrief and discuss...
The high achievers in the game were probably the risk-takers.
*Do we as managers of people take enough positive risks with them? For example, do we trust them with enough responsibility to develop them professionally, or do we err on the safe side? Are we over-reluctant to delegate important tasks and goals? Do we do too much for them? Do we over-support as opposed to challenge? Do we allow them enough space to act on their own initiatives? In difficult situations do we take over too soon?*
*(Allow about 30 minutes for a full discussion)*

4 *Action task...*Give each participant a piece of paper and ask them to write down the names of their department staff on it. (*This simple procedure helps to clear minds and focus attention.*)
Ask them to study the names and ask themselves the following questions:
*Which of these people can take on more responsibility than they currently have?*

Which of these people is ready to be entrusted with developing a new initiative within the department? If they face any doubts, suggest they ask themselves the following question:
*If I risk it, what is the worst that can happen?*
If they could live with the worst scenario, the risk is likely to be worth taking!
(*About 15 minutes for this and further discussion*)

---

## In the classroom...

Use the *Risk it!* game with older pupils as a stimulus to discussions about risk taking. Do they tend to not go for things/challenges because of their fear of failure or fear of looking small in the eyes of their peers?
Think of specifics to focus the discussion upon: *I like the look of this job... no... I don't stand a chance, so I won't apply!... I'd like to ask Annie to the Disco... no... she doesn't fancy me! etc*

Key skills sheets 3 and 5

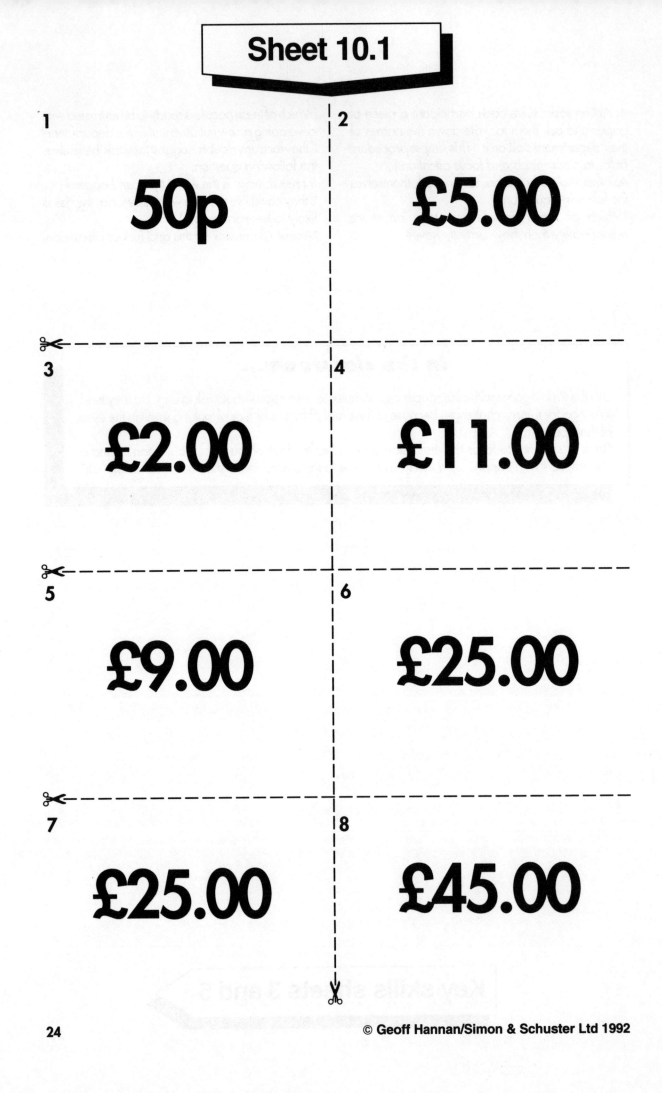

1

# 50p

2

# £5.00

3

# £2.00

4

# £11.00

5

# £9.00

6

# £25.00

7

# £25.00

8

# £45.00

9

# £100.00

10

# £5.00

11

# £150.00

12

# £1,000.00

13

# Nothing!

14

# Nothing!

15

# Nothing!

16

# Nothing!

# Activity 11 Assert Yourself!

Many people find it difficult to be assertive (the exercise below defines the term). It is a key skill for managers (and everyone else?) to acquire, since it is fundamentally about being honest and respectful in one's dealings with others. To paraphrase Goethe: if you treat people as if they were what they ought to be, you help them to become what they are capable of being!

I have used the following exercise to great effect in analysing the specifics of the assertive skills that individual managers need. As you'll see, it's a bold exercise! It can be a lot of fun, but it needs a trainer who *is* assertive and who feels on top of their subject matter. If you think you can handle it, you probably can – and it provides for a memorable training session!

## Objectives

To define assertive behaviour
To focus participants on the importance of assertive managerial practices

## Target group

All management levels

*Whole group* individual and pair work

## Duration

About one and a half hours

## Materials

One stick of celery for each participant!
Paper and pens
A copy of Sheet 11.1 *Behaviours* for each participant.

## Operation

1 Assemble the participants behind tables, facing you.

2 Without explanation, give each a sheet of paper.

3 Introduce the session as follows:
*In this session we are going to examine an important aspect of management... the wrapping of celery. I am going to give each person here a stick of celery. I am going to allow you just 30 minutes to wrap that stick of celery in the piece of paper you have in front of you.* (Give each person a stick of celery.)
*Your time starts now.*
Get out a newspaper and read it! Allow time for reactions to develop. Refuse to answer any questions.
(*Five to ten minutes is usually enough!*)

4 Debrief as follows...
*The absurd task was likely to provoke one of four reactions...*
● *Passive. You could have sat there wrapping your piece of celery without having the slightest idea why you were doing it. Or you could have decided it was a ridiculous thing to do and just sat there doing nothing.*
● *Aggressive. You might have told me aggressively what you thought about my silly task. You could even have walked out.*
● *Manipulative. You might have become disaffected and roused a group of people around you, egging on a rebellion against me!*
● *Assertive. You could have calmly expressed your discontent with the activity and asked my reasons for setting it. This response credits me with some integrity behind what was apparently a stupid assignment.*

5 Give out the copies of Sheet 11.1 *Behaviours*...
Take the group sequentially through its sections, relating it to their own experiences. This may be done quite simply by asking after each type of behaviour described if they can think of someone who fits the bill!

Spend a little time examining the benefits of the 'good management practice' statements at the bottom of the sheet. You could perhaps get them to brainstorm the efficacy of the approaches stated. (*20 minutes*)

6 Divide the group into pairs and give each pair a sheet of paper. Ask them to invent a scenario entitled 'a difficult professional situation'. The scenario should involve a problem with a 'subordinate' which is potentially difficult to handle. They should explain the situation they have invented concisely and explicitly so that another pair can understand it without needing to ask questions. (*15 minutes*)

7 *Action task* Ask pairs to swap their scenarios. Working on the new scenario they have received, ask them to devise a 'solution scenario' for the manager to deal with the problem.

This should be a totally assertive response to the situation and comply with the 'good management practice' statement presented at the end of Sheet 11.1.
(*15 minutes*)

8 Share the problem and solution scenarios. Highlight the process used in section 6 above: prior to dealing with a real problem, first analyse it in detail. An effective way of doing this is to write notes that first detail how *you* perceive the situation but also seek to analyse how the other party might perceive it. From here you can go on to examine possible causes and possible actions. (See Key Skills Sheet 4).
(*20 minutes or so depending on size of group*)

## In the classroom...

Assertive training for young people builds confidence and explores new options in their dealings with peers and adults. You could use the 'Assertive people' sheet to focus the students' minds on the times they are too passive, manipulative and aggressive. They could describe situations from their own experience and suggest 'assertive' alternatives to their responses. Using role play to try out the assertive behaviours can be very effective in teaching the skills needed.

## Key skills sheet 4

# Behaviours

**Passive behaviour** is characterised by:
- avoidance of responsibility
- a fear of causing offence
- moaning/blaming of others
- projection of self as a victim
- a negative response to things
- always seeking advice
- guilt feelings
- feelings of not being in control
- inability to take risks

**Aggressive behaviour** is characterised by:
- seeming hostile and antagonistic
- over-reacting to things
- seeming selfish
- easily alienating others
- a refusal to accept criticism
- being a rebel-rouser
- moodiness
- an inability to take steps to remedy things
- resorting to verbal abuse
- inability to openly express feelings of resentment
- seeking to prove superiority

**Assertive behaviour** is characterised by:
- ability to express feelings honestly and openly
- ability to communicate needs to others
- confidence in own abilities
- respectful treatment of others
- ability to accept opposing views
- not needing to put others down
- being in control of choices and options
- ability to accept short-comings in others
- risk-taking

**Manipulative behaviour** is characterised by:
- attempting to make others feel guilty
- presenting confusing messages to people
- conveying disapproval covertly
- hiding feelings of vulnerability
- reluctance to commit themselves
- seeking to manoeuvre things to their own advantage
- frequent flattery
- skilful deceit
- being disloyal

**Good management practice** is...
- always expressing openly yet sensitively your feelings towards others
- being willing to compromise to find the best possible solution for all concerned
- openly inviting constructive criticism of your actions and openly inviting other people's opinions on your management methods
- having considered all sides to an argument and considered the feelings of others, being able to make unpopular decisions that you know are the best ones. (Being able to clearly define your reasons.)
- being open and honest in your dealings with others
- being able to admit when you're wrong or have made a mistake

# Section Two: Working together in teams

'Come on!' said number one
'After you!' said number two
'I don't agree!' said number three
'It's such a bore!' said number four
'We won't survive!' said number five
'We're in a fix!' said number six
'This way to heaven!' said number seven
'It's far too late' said number eight
'There's plenty of time!' said number nine
'Late again!' said number ten

Let's play Follow the Leader!

# Activity 12 The Ladder Game

I devised the following game as a way of introducing Senior Managers to 'Management of change' theory. It facilitates discussion on a dozen or so key factors to take into account when planning for change.

## Objectives

To explore some planning components in the management of change
To facilitate discussion upon good management of change practice

## Target group

Senior Management

*Group work* Groups of three

## Duration

About one and a half hours

## Materials

A copy of Sheet 12.1 *Ladder* (enlarged to A3) and a counter for each group
A copy of Sheet 12.2 *Debrief sheet* for yourself
A copy of *Key skills sheet 7* (at the back of the book) for each participant
Paper and pens

## Operation

1  Divide participants into groups of three and ask them to brainstorm 12 things major change might do to an organisation and its employees. At this stage you want them to look at general effects of change in the abstract. Allow just ten minutes.

2  Ask the groups to invent, as a model to work on, a major policy/practice change for their school (or, indeed, select a major change they actually wish to facilitate).
(*Ten minutes*)

3  Set the following task...
*You wish this change to take effect in 12 calendar months from now. You have 30 minutes to plan what you need to do between now and your target date. You may find that starting points are suggested by the brainstorm you did... ie what do you need to do to enhance the good effects you outlined and mitigate the bad effects?*
(*Allow 30 minutes*)

4  Give each group a copy of the *Ladder* (Sheet 12.1) and a counter. Ask them to put their counter on the starting point highlighted. Explain how the game works...

*The desired developmental level in 12 months time is represented by rung 12 on the ladder. To achieve this development you will have needed, in the 12 months preceding, to have satisfied certain criteria for the successful management of change.*
*I am going to read out the criteria and see if you have taken them into account in your planning. If you have, you will be able to move your counter smoothly up the ladder. If not, you may find yourself stuck or be asked to move down a rung.*

5  Ask groups to tell you what their desired change is. Read out the debrief sheet, discussing each item in turn. People take the game very seriously and you'll find them keen to progress to the top of the ladder. Be lenient on them!
(*About 30 minutes*)

6  Give out copies of *Key skills sheet 7* and take them briefly through the checklist.

7  *Action task* Suggest they could apply the checklist on *Key skills sheet 7* to a current developmental initiative, large or small. It might suggest something else that could be done to consolidate and further develop the initiatives already undertaken.

## Key skills sheet 7

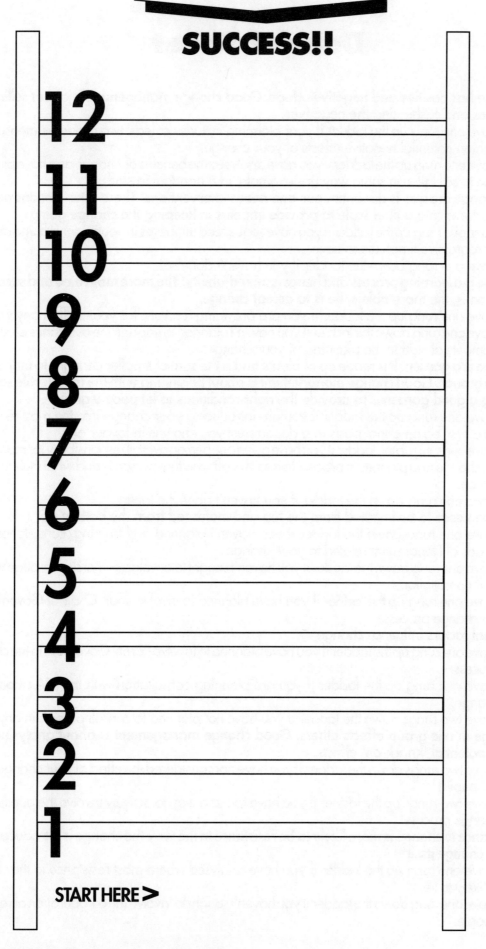

# Debrief Sheet

1  **Change has positive and negative effects. Good change management is about selling the positives and cushioning the negatives.**
   - Move one rung *up* the ladder if your planning includes at least two proactive measures to cushion potential negative effects of your change.
   - Move one rung *up* the ladder if you have analysed the benefits of change and have planned time to sell these in some way (for example, in a handout to staff).

2  **The change process is discontinuous and needs interventions. These interventions need to be structured into a time scale to provide impetus in keeping the change going.**
   - Move one rung *up* the ladder if you have sequenced initiatives in your planning and applied a progressive timescale to each.
   - Move one rung *down* the ladder if you haven't done so!

3  **Change is a learning process and hence is mixed-ability! The more motivated and successful a person is, the more able s/he is to accept change.**
   - Move one rung *up* the ladder if you are providing 'carrots' for your staff in any way.
   - Move one rung *down* the ladder if you haven't planned to engage the assistance of selected members of staff in the planning of your change.

4  **Change is a garden. It is made up of plants and is the sum of smaller changes to individuals and to groups. Good change management is about beginning with the most fertile soil and having a good gardener to provide the right conditions to let people grow!**
   - Move one rung *up* the ladder if you are introducing your change into the most receptive area first, eg on a trial basis in a department you know is in favour of it.
   - Move one rung *up* the ladder if you have given *one* person overall responsibility for managing the change and planned a process to inform staff who that person is and what their function will be.
   - Move one rung *down* the ladder if you haven't done the latter!

5  **Change needs to be initiated from the top and managed from the bottom up.**
   - Move one rung *down* the ladder if you haven't planned any training/consultation with Heads of Department related to your change.
   - Move one rung *down* the ladder if you haven't sought to develop ownership through whole-staff consultation.
   - Move one rung *up* the ladder if you have planned to involve your Chair of Governors in the change process.

6  **External factors influence change**
   - Move one rung *up* the ladder if you have planned to involve Parent Governors in the change process.
   - Move one rung *up* the ladder if you are planning consultation with the LEA about your change.
   - Move two rungs *down* the ladder if you have not planned to consult parents in any way!

7  **Change in one group affects others. Good change management is about analysing and using potential 'knock-on' effects.**
   - Move two rungs *down* the ladder if you have not considered the effect of your change upon the pupils!
   - Move two rungs *up* the ladder if you have found a way to actively involve the pupils in the change process.

8  **Resistance to change is more likely to be resistance to the way the change is introduced than to the change itself!**
   - Move one rung *up* the ladder if you have analysed where most resistance to the change is likely to lie.
   - Move one rung *down* the ladder if you haven't sought to involve the co-operation of resistant people.

# Activity 13 20/80

I'm sure you won't disagree with me when I say that one of the biggest problems for managers in education is volume of workload! Time management systems are not a cure-all but many teachers have found the following useful in posing fundamental questions about how they use their precious time. Some have even taken steps to alleviate the problem!

The title, by the way, refers to the fact that probably 20 per cent of what you do produces 80 per cent of the results...

## Objective

To evaluate use of managerial time

## Target group

Senior Management

*Solo work* and group discussion

## Duration

One hour

## Materials

One copy of Sheet 13.1 *Diary* per participant
Paper and pens

## Operation

1  Give each person a sheet of paper and ask them to write a brief Mission Statement... a few lines on what they perceive their working objectives to be.
(*Ten minutes*)

2  Give each a copy of the *Diary* (Sheet 13.1). Ask them to complete it as instructed.
(*About ten minutes*)

3  Instruct them as follows:
*Look back at your Mission Statement. Now, in column 2, enter a score for each of the day's activities, on a scale of 0–3. 3 means the activity was of fundamental importance to the fulfilling of the mission; 2 means it was important; 1 means it was of little importance; and 0 of no importance whatever.*
(*Ten minutes*)

4  Ask participants to add up the number of activities in column 1 and multiply the answer by three. Explain:
*The difference between this and the total score in column 2 will indicate the fraction of time you spend on activities that – in an ideal world – you shouldn't be doing at all!*
(*Five minutes*)

5  But – as someone is likely to point out – we don't live in an ideal world. So, ask participants to fill in column 3 by putting 'R' for 'Reactive' against all the activities that were unplanned spontaneous ones.
(*Five minutes*)

6  Continue: *Now, in column 4, put an 'L' by any activities that you would really like to 'lose', or think you should.*
(*Five minutes*)

7  Suggest that the secret of better time management is to find a way of minimising the low-scoring 'R' activities and trying to get rid of all the 'L's. Discuss how this might be done.

Some good suggestions normally come out of the discussion... The best way to reduce the 'R's can be through the creation of 'handling' systems and increased proactivity in planning. The 'L's might be handled through delegation.

8  *Action task* Challenge participants to try out an idea or two from the above discussion.

## Key skills sheet 3

## Diary

In Column 1, note down all the activities you undertook yesterday (or on your last day at work).

|  | 1 | 2 | 3 | 4 |
|---|---|---|---|---|
| 08.00 |  |  |  |  |
| 09.00 |  |  |  |  |
| 10.00 |  |  |  |  |
| 11.00 |  |  |  |  |
| 12.00 |  |  |  |  |
| 13.00 |  |  |  |  |
| 14.00 |  |  |  |  |
| 15.00 |  |  |  |  |
| 16.00 |  |  |  |  |
| 17.00 |  |  |  |  |
| 18.00 |  |  |  |  |

# Activity 14 Bin It!

It is eight o'clock in the morning. You arrive at school. You have 20 separate things to do this morning (plus, of course, classes to teach!) What do you do first? How do you avoid the nervous breakdown that seems scheduled for morning break!?

Ask any Middle Manager in Education what is their biggest professional concern and they will tell you of the heavy workload they are under. Time management systems can provide some signposts through the maze. Here's a simple system, introduced in a wonderfully therapeutic way, ideal for a training session after a hectic day!

## Objectives

To teach an approach to 'task separation'
To promote discussion on the most effective use of managerial time
To promote discussion on delegation

## Target group

Middle Managers, but equally useful with Senior Managers

*Pair work* then into small groups

## Duration

About one hour in all

## Materials

Four wastebins, labelled from the viewer's left in sequence:
1 **Urgent and Important**
2 **Important but not Urgent**
3 **Urgent but not Important**
4 **Not Urgent and not Important**
Some sheets of lined A4 paper and pens
A copy of Sheet 14.1 for each participant

## Operation

1 Divide participants into pairs and give each pair a sheet of paper. Instruct them as follows:
*On the sheet list ten common tasks you perform as Head of Department. Leave an empty line between each task.*
(*About 15 minutes*)

2 Produce the wastebins, labelled as above. Place them on a table in sequence in front of the group. Instruct the group as follows:
*Tear up your sheet and assign each of your ten tasks to their appropriate bin! Discuss each task in turn with your partner and make your decisions sequentially.*
Sit back and enjoy the smiles you see as they post their tasks in the bin!
(*15 minutes*)

3 Assemble the group. Take a few slips of paper from each of the bins in turn. Read them out. Don't spend long on discussion at this stage. Ask the group for a couple of examples of where they found bin allocation difficult.

4 Ask participants to form groups of four. Give each person a copy of Sheet 14.1. Allow them 15 minutes to discuss the proposition presented on the top of the sheet and the categories in the boxes. Invite spokespersons to report back on the feelings of each group.

5 *Action task...* Ask participants to use the grid over the coming week, noting down each managerial task under its appropriate heading before doing it or delegating it. (Ideally alot some time during your next training session to debrief this.) Ask them to really give the system a fair trial, despite any reservations they might have. Used with increasing expertise in the assignment of tasks it proves a very effective time management tool.

## In the classroom...

You can use the *Bin-it!* game in a number of ways with young people. In PSE, for example, you could get them to analyse typical adolescent concerns and bin them, as a stimulus to discussing priorities important for them individually. With a Year 11 group this could evolve into a study-management system. It's equally useful in looking at specifics, eg *You have an interview coming up; list the things you need to do in preparation and put them in the appropriate bin.*

Key skills sheet 3

The art of effective time management is about doing the Important and delegating the Urgent.

Practically, this should work as follows...

| | |
|---|---|
| **Urgent and Important**<br>Do yourself *now* but ensure that in the future important things are planned for in advance, wherever possible. | **Important but not Urgent**<br>Plan a sensible deadline for doing this yourself. |
| **Urgent but not Important**<br>Delegate this to somebody else. Delegate the responsibility for doing this sort of thing to somebody else. | **Not Urgent and not Important**<br>Does it really need to be done at all? If it does, you really shouldn't be the one to do it! |

# Activity 15 Patterns

Effective team work is of obvious importance at all levels of management. Sharing the 'mission' of the organisation is the key to getting a group of individuals with different experience, expertise and understandings to work towards shared objectives. This easily set-up game, with accompanying worksheets, provides a dynamic focus for exploring whether team members do indeed share the same mission and operate effective organisational support structures to achieve it!

The activity here is aimed at Senior Managers. I shall make the assumption that the Senior Team referred to consists of a Head, Three Deputies and Four Senior Teachers.

The activity can be easily adapted for smaller teams. The following activity (16) shows an adaptation for Middle Management.

## Objectives

To explore the need for sharing the same mission
To analyse key organisational structures and evaluate their efficacy

## Target group

Senior Management

*Small groups*

## Duration

One and a half hours

## Materials

One copy of Sheet 15.1 *Letter square* enlarged to A3
Two copies of Sheet 15.2 *Mission support* enlarged onto A3 and cut into four sections as indicated
A sheet of A3 paper per group

## Operation

1 Divide the group into two teams: Heads and Deputies *versus* Senior Teachers. Each team should be seated around a separate table with another, empty table between them. With a small group, run the challenge below against the clock...

2 Give each group a sheet of A3 paper. Place the enlarged *Letter square* (Sheet 15.1) on the table between the teams. Explain the task:
*On the central table is a diagram containing squares with letters in them. Your task is to reproduce this diagram exactly on the blank sheet in front of you. Two further rules... 1. The sheet on which you are reproducing the diagram may at no time be moved from your team's table. Nor may the central sheet be moved. 2. Only one team member at a time may visit the central table to look at the diagram and that team member may only stay at the table for ten seconds. The first team to accurately reproduce the diagram is the winner!*
(*About 20 minutes*)

3 Debrief as follows..
To achieve the task certain things were necessary:
• *That you were all working to shared objectives. You all needed to share the 'mission'. If one team member was disinterested, for example, and when at the table didn't take time and effort to faithfully relay the contents of the diagram, the whole team would have lost!*
• *To function at its optimum level 'task separation' could have been a useful way of working. One person might be especially good at remembering patterns, another a good draftsperson, another a good organiser/time keeper, yet another good at evaluating where the competitors were up to and so on.*
• *Fully understanding the task and its complexities prior to starting was important.*
• *Analysis of possible methods and working out a system prior to starting the challenge could have saved time in the long run.*

4 Give each group the first section of the enlarged Sheet 15.2 – *Mission support*. Ask them to complete it.
(*Ten to 15 minutes*)

5 Give each group the second section of the enlarged Sheet 15.2. Ask them to lay it alongside the first section and complete it.
(*Ten to 15 minutes*)

6 Give each group the third section; ask them to lay it alongside and complete it.

They have now been taken sequentially through an analysis of how well their shared objectives translate into effective managerial support. Compare and contrast the work of the groups. Discuss ways they might collaborate more effectively in their management roles.

7 *Action task* Bring the two groups together to discuss ways their managerial support structures may be improved. Invite them to draft a statement to complete the sentence on the final section of the *Mission support* sheet (15.2) (or they could do this after the session).

A good starting point for discussion is to refer back to the *Letter square* game and explore with them if they are using the different skills and team members to best advantage. Then look at the two teams' mission objectives to see if there are any noticeable differences.

## In the classroom...

The copying-the-grid idea can be used in exactly the same way to stimulate discussion on good group work. Play the game with pupils as a contest and then get them to discuss how they could have performed the task more effectively (pre-planning etc). They'll probably want to play it again, so have another, more difficult grid ready!

**Key skills sheets 5 and 6**

# Sheet 15.1

## Patterns

| | | | | | | | START HERE | | | |
|---|---|---|---|---|---|---|---|---|---|---|
| O | D | O | O | G | ← | → | | C | T | |
| R | | | T | E | A | M | | E | I | S |
| G | | | W | O | R | K | | J | V | N |
| A | | | | A | N | D | ↓ | B | E | O |
| N | | | | | | | | O | S | I |
| I | | | | | | | G | | | T |
| Z | | | | | | | N | | | P |
| A | | | | | | | I | R | I | E |
| T | | | | | | | R | A | N | C |
| I | | | | | | | A | H | G | R |
| O | ▼ | | | | | | H | S | | E |
| N | D | E | M | A | N | DS | 1 | S | 2 | + | P |

# Mission Support

Each arrow ◄ indicates that the statement relates specifically to the statement in the previous column.

| **1** The mission of our school is... | **2** In our role as senior management we support the mission by... | **3** We facilitate other staff to support the mission by... |
|---|---|---|
| 1 | ◄ 1 | ◄ 1 |
| 2 | ◄ 2 | ◄ 2 |
| 3 | ◄ 3 | ◄ 3 |
| 4 | ◄ 4 | ◄ 4 |
| 5 | ◄ 5 | ◄ 5 |

✂ ─────────────────────────────────

To improve our working towards shared objectives we could... _____

_____

_____

_____

_____

# Activity 16 Thought Experiment

Using metaphor or simile is a natural linguistic process that helps us to understand concepts. For example, the metaphor of water is used in economics (cash flow, currency, bank etc). A similar process may be used to good effect in training to provide a focus for exploration. We frequently understand something better in the context of something else!

In this activity 'thought experiment' and metaphor help to focus the participants' attention on the potential of their influence within their organisation. A dynamic organisation, of course, will seek to maximise the involvement and participation of its employees, to create a rich 'culture' for itself....

## Objectives

To explore the participants' potential influence upon the school
To target developments in their influence

## Target group

Middle managers

*Small groups* of four

## Duration

An hour and a half

## Materials

A copy of Sheet 16.1 *Scenario* for each group, (divided in two)
A copy of Sheet 16.2 *Planets* for each group
A copy of Sheet 16.3 *Spheres of influence* for each participant
Pens and paper

## Operation

1 Ask participants to form groups of four. Give each group a copy of Sheet 16.1 Part A. Allow them 10 minutes to complete the task.

2 Give out copies of Sheet 16.1 Part B. Allow groups 15 minutes to reach a solution.

3 Share each group's solution, getting the other groups to vote on whether or not they satisfy the criteria!
(*About ten minutes*)

4 Debrief...
*The above activity has generated a lot of fun and a considerable amount of creative thought and communication, especially about finding connections...*
*People in any organisation are interconnected and have a direct or indirect effect upon one-another. Part of a Manager's job is to manage these connections for maximum benefit to the whole.*
*A metaphor for this process is a solar system where the gravitational influences of the sun and the planets keep everything in equilibrium and motion. Imagine as Head of Department that you are the sun at the centre of all these gravitational influences, your solar system might look something like this...*
Give each group a copy of Sheet 16.2 *Planets*.

5 Ask them as a group to fill in the sheet as directed. You'll find that the lead-in activities have had a significant effect on the quality of the analysis.
(*About 30 minutes*)

6 Bring the groups together to compare and contrast their diagrams.
(*20 minutes*)

7 *Action task* Give participants a copy of Sheet 16.3 *Spheres of influence* to take away for detailed consideration and completion. You could discuss this at your next training session. As a Senior Manager you could use the content as a starting point for supporting their developmental initiatives.

**Key skills sheets 3 and 5**

# Scenario

## Part A

Planet Earth is doomed. A group of hyper-intelligent aliens from another galaxy have selected the four of you to be the sole survivors. They have provided you with an uninhabited planet to live on, similar in every respect to Earth. They have also provided you with a space craft to get you there.

The aliens are allowing each of you to take one human skill from the accumulated wisdom of Humanity. Your task is to select the four human skills to take on your trip. (They could be interpersonal, managerial, practical etc in nature.) They should be selected on the basis of having most influence on the quality of your future life on your new planet. Each one of you will have a skill thought-transplanted into you. You have ten minutes to select the skills you will take and enter them below.

| Name | Skill |
|------|-------|
| 1 _____ | _____ |
| 2 _____ | _____ |
| 3 _____ | _____ |
| 4 _____ | _____ |

- - - - - - - - - - - - - - - - - - - - - - - - - - - - - - - - - ✂

## Part B

You have left Planet Earth and are travelling through space towards your destination. Suddenly a message comes through from the aliens. Owing to cut-backs in spending they are rethinking giving you the planet to colonise. They are thinking of using it themselves for dumping waste, a problem they have no expertise in handling.

By using the skills you have taken with you, you are able to influence their decision brilliantly by presenting them with a mutually-useful solution. BUT you must use all the skills you have taken with you, indicating a clear significance for each in the solution you suggest! Each person will thus need to defend the appropriateness of their chosen skill to the solution of the problem. You have 15 minutes to formulate your solution.

# Planets

**Senior Management**

Current whole-school priorities:

1
2
3

1
2
3
4
5

Influence

**You**

1
2
3
4
5

**Your Department**

Current priorities:

1
2
3

## INSTRUCTIONS

a) In the 'Senior Management' and 'Your Department' boxes, define three priorities you are currently focusing on as a whole school and as a department.

b) On the 'influence' lines, define five areas where you feel you have major influence on Senior Management/whole school issues and on the Department. (The priorities in the circles may provide a useful starting-point for this analysis.)

44

© Geoff Hannan/Simon & Schuster Ltd 1992

# Spheres of influence

What areas of whole school policy do you feel you already have influence upon?

_____

_____

What steps can you take to enhance and develop your current spheres of influence?

_____

_____

What areas of policy would you like to have more influence upon?

_____

_____

Why?

_____

_____

What specifically do you feel you have to offer?

_____

_____

With what practical outcomes?

_____

_____

With which members of the organisation do you need to develop links to achieve greater influence in the above area?

_____

_____

Would you anticipate resistance to your increased influence and, if so, why?

_____

_____

How might you endeavour to diminish this resistance?

_____

_____

# Activity 17 It's Your Funeral!*

This is an outline of another activity based on the idea of 'guided fantasy'. Develop the storyline and relate it fluently.

## Objective

To encourage people to think about the importance of defining their own professional 'mission'.

## Target group

All management levels

*Solo work* followed by whole group discussion

## Duration

About one hour

## Materials

Pens and paper

## Operation

1  Read out the following story:
*It's five years from now. You are going to a funeral. You don't know whose funeral it is. You find yourself at the church. It's a misty, Autumnal evening (embroider as you like!). The church is packed with mourners...*

*Suddenly you realise whose funeral it is – it's your own! Someone from school gets up to deliver a speech all about you. It's wonderful! Full of warmly-delivered compliments about your professionalism and your dynamic personal qualities that will be so much missed in the school. Three particular phrases keep reappearing in the speech...*

2  Get participants to write down, individually, what they would like these phrases to be. These phrases will reflect a wonderful mixture of integrity and egotism!

3  Suggest that these phrases might form the basis for a very practical mission statement, ie 'I'd like people to see me like this and I want my work to be appreciated like this: how can I work towards it?' Share and discuss with the whole group.

4  *Action task* Invite participants to write their own mission statements. The statement should be no more than a page in length. It should sum up philosophy and objectives, be something they can easily transmit to others and also evaluate their own performance against.

Ask participants to think about where they want to be in five years' time. What promotion will they seek? What do they need to do to manage their own professional development?

*Adapted from an idea by Stephen R Covey (see Suggested Reading)

# Activity 18 Tammy Tiller's Testimonial

## Objective

To encourage discussion on leadership skills

## Target group

Middle Management

*Pair work* followed by whole group discussion

## Duration

About one hour

## Materials

Paper and pens

## Operation

1  Read out the following story:
*Tammy is Head of Maths in a Comprehensive School and has been so for many years. She is loved by everyone – children, colleagues and parents alike. Through her, the Maths department achieves excellent results. Now Tammy is retiring. The two of you have to write the farewell speech for her retirement dinner. She is a dynamic woman with a low boredom threshold – the speech must not last more than two minutes and in it you must sum up her qualities of leadership.*

2  Get participants to form pairs and write the speech.

3  Reassemble the group and ask the pairs to read out their speeches. Invite comment from the rest of the group and note recurring themes for discussion. This a good way of getting the group to focus on their own values, before going on to quantify them more objectively.

4  In the debrief, concentrate on: 'This is how we want to be... how do we achieve it within our own departments?'

5  *Action task* Ask each participant to target a short-term development in their leadership approach: for example, giving more one-to-one time or planning a programme of development for a team member.

**Key skills sheet 5**

# Activity 19 What's your role?

Our own perceptions of our role in an organisation and the perceptions of others have an important bearing upon 'role performance' – how well we do and are seen to do our job. As a middle manager, I might not perceive that I have a staff counselling role, but my boss might. She might assess my performance partly upon the counselling work I don't do! More importantly, if I haven't analysed my role and the demands of my job, how will I be able to assess my own performance and plan for my own development? As well as giving you a way-in to discussing this important theme, the following exercise also illustrates the 'outer-circle/inner circle' method of group work, a very useful training device and a useful team work tool.

## Objectives

To explore the participants' professional roles
To target their developmental needs

## Target group

Middle Managers

*Small groups* of six or less. You must have an even number of groups, so size them accordingly.

## Duration

About one and a half hours

## Materials

A copy of Sheet 19.1 *Roles* per group, copied onto sticky labels
A copy of Sheet 19.2 *Role analysis* per participant
Pens and paper

## Operation

1  Divide into an equal number of groups, of equal size. I'll assume for the instructions below you are working with just two groups of six, the 'A' group and the 'B' group. (For larger numbers of participants, label the groups 1A/1B, 2A/2B etc)

2  Give each group a copy of Sheet 19.1 *Roles*. Explain how the Outer Circle/Inner Circle task works...
*I shall give a task to the 'A' group. During the task the 'B' group will observe them.*
*Following this I shall give a different task to the 'B' group and the 'A' group will do the observing.*

3  Ask both groups to prepare as follows...
*During your group's task, each team member must perform within the confines of a 'Role'. The Role Sheet contains labels defining the individual roles available. As a team, select the roles you feel would be most useful in achieving any discussion-based task. Each person in the group is allowed to have just one label and hence play just one role within the team.*
Allow ten minutes for groups to choose roles and decide who will play each.

4  Ask them to remove the labels selected from the *Role* sheet and stick them on the individuals who will be playing them. Reinforce that this label describes the role they must play during the group work task. Tell them that the other team will be assessing them on how well they play this role!

5  Ask the 'B' group to move over to the 'A' group. Ask each 'B' group member to select one member of the 'A' group to assess (allow a couple of minutes for them to organise this). Give a sheet of paper and a pen to each 'B' group member and instruct them as follows:
*During the task I am about to give Group A, study your colleague and assess how well they are fulfilling the role described on their label. Note how well they use their role within the group, if they deviate from it, etc. You will debrief your observations with them afterwards.*

6 Get the 'B' group to form an outer circle around the 'A' group. Remind them that they are to act as observers. Set the 'A' group the following task.

(Any puzzle-based task will do here. Should anyone in the 'A' group know the solution, you could substitute the task in section 8 – or have one of your own ready as a fall-back.)

*Janet and John are ten-year-old twins. Whenever mealtimes come and cake is for dessert, there is an argument over who has the bigger half of the cake. Dad could measure the halves with a tape measure in front of them to no avail... one would always claim it wasn't fair as the other had a bigger half. Mum is Headteacher of a primary school Understanding children's natural sense of justice, she hit upon an ingenious way of stopping these arguments. They still get their cake, but now eat it without complaint. What did clever Mum do? You have 15 minutes to discuss possibilities and decide on a solution.*
(Solution at the end)

7 Stop the activity. Ask the 'A' group to share their solution. Then get the 'B' group members to share their assessments of the 'A' group's respective performances.
(*Allow ten minutes*)

8 Repeat with 'A' group now in the outer circle assessing the 'B' group on the following task:

*A judge sentences a prisoner to be executed one day next week. He also demands that the prisoner should not know which day the execution is going to take place. The prisoner, a genius in logic, knows he cannot therefore be executed... Why?*
(*Allow 15 minutes*)

9 Stop the activity. Ask the 'B' group to share their solution and the 'A' group their assessments. You now have a very strong experiential base to focus discussion on the importance of close role definitions both for themselves and others in their department.

10 Explain the parallel between the task they've been involved in and good teamwork, which is frequently optimised by close role definition within the team.

Discuss:
- *The importance of the Head of Department's role definition and its dissemination to the team – so that others know with whom specific responsibilities lie and the extent of their own autonomy, ie what is and is not the job of the HoD.*
- *The importance of our own 'role perception' in evaluating our success, ie defining our own strengths and weaknesses relative to the job.*
- *How we can use both the above in targeting areas of development for ourselves and our subordinates.*
(*Ten minutes*)
- *How they can use both the above in targeting areas of development for themselves and their subordinates.*
(*At least 30 minutes*)

11 Suggest how the outer-circle/inner-circle technique could be used in department meetings to explore developmental ideas:
*You can structure discussions so that half the group engage directly in the discussion process and the other half take up an observational role; noting down points omitted and ideas that occur to them through just listening. Sharing these observations will frequently produce a far richer exploration of ideas and possibilities.*

12 *Action task* Give each participant a copy of Sheet 19.2 *Role analysis*. Ask them to take some time over the coming week to complete the worksheet.
(Suggest that they bring it back to your next training session and if a Senior Manager, contract support for them in meeting their own developmental targets.)

*Answer to puzzle A*
Mum now alternates giving one twin the knife to cut the cake in two and the other the first choice in selecting their half.

*Answer to puzzle B*
He cannot be executed on the last day of next week because on the day preceding it he would know what day he would be executed. Nor can he be executed on the second from last day, because being now effectively the last possible day, the same logic applies. And so on to the start of the week! (Think about it!).

## *In the classroom...*

Both the role-labelling process (in a simplified form) and the outer/inner circle technique can be used to good effect in getting young people to explore group work practices.

**HEADTEACHER**

Please knock

○ ENTER
○ WAIT
○ ENGAGED
○ COME BACK
NEXT TERM

**Key skills sheet 5 and 6**

# Roles

### Facilitator
*Role*: To facilitate the discussion process

### Questioner
*Role*: To question positively

### Arguer
*Role*: Devil's Advocate

### Ideas person
*Role*: To present ideas for exploration by the team, not to evaluate them

### Time keeper
*Role*: To ensure optimum use of the time available

### Assimilator
*Role*: To note and recap periodically upon ideas presented

### Joker
*Role*: To ensure everyone enjoys the task

### Empiricist
*Role*: To accept or reject ideas solely upon grounds of own personal experience

### Judge
*Role*: To make objective decisions on the ideas presented

### Pragmatist
*Role*: To reject or accept suggestions on grounds of practicality

### Artist
*Role*: To look for the unusual

### Moralist
*Role*: To select or reject ideas on grounds of integrity

# Role analysis

I perceive my primary functions as team leader as being...

1 _____

2 _____

3 _____

4 _____

5 _____

1  I fulfil function one by _____

_____

I could improve it by _____

_____

2  I fulfil function two by _____

_____

I could improve it by _____

_____

3  I fulfil function three by _____

_____

I could improve it by _____

_____

4  I fulfil function four by _____

_____

I could improve it by _____

_____

5  I fulfil function five by _____

_____

I could improve it by _____

- - - - - - - - - - - - - - - - - - - - - - - - - - - -

I disseminate my functions to my team by _____

_____

I could improve this dissemination by _____

_____

# Activity 20 What's missing?

This activity uses the same outer circle/inner circle technique as the previous exercise and the same labels (Sheet 19.1) to focus on the developmental needs of the participants' team as a whole. Participating HoDs could usefully run the activity in its entirety within their departments.

## Objectives

To assess their team's developmental needs as a team unit
To target improvements

## Target group

Middle Management

*Small groups* as in the last activity

## Duration

One and a half hours

## Materials

A copy of Sheet 19.1 *Roles* (from Activity 19) per group
A copy of Sheet 20.1 *Team development* per participant

## Operation

Follow instructions 1 to 9 as in the previous activity, then...
10 Ask each group to reform separately and decide which of the roles they did *not* select (from Sheet 19.1) would have been most useful in improving their collective performance during the tasks.
(*Ten minutes*)

This now shifts the experiential benefits of the activity's focus in a different direction...

11 Discuss...
• *Good team work is about merging different individual talents into a unit where working together they are more effectual than any of the individuals could be in working alone. Hence, some tasks are more appropriate than others for team work. (Changing the proverbial lightbulb isn't!)*
• *Good team work demands the defining of roles within the team so the unit works together at its optimum effectiveness. (Having five generals and one soldier equals defeat!)*
• *Looking for 'holes' in the talents and operation of the team is an effective starting point for evaluating a team's developmental needs.*

12 *Action task* Give each participant a copy of Sheet 20.1 *Team development* and ask them to spend some time during the coming week completing the worksheet. Or they might like to engage their department in its completion; perhaps cascading the above activities as part of their own team training.

**Key skills sheet 6**

# Team development

**A**  Evaluate below the main strengths of your team.

1 _____

2 _____

3 _____

4 _____

**B**  For each of the above note a way in which you might consolidate, enhance or develop that strength.

1 _____

2 _____

3 _____

4 _____

**C**  Evaluate below two weaknesses of your team.

1 _____

2 _____

**D**  For each of the above target a short-term development to mitigate or compensate for the weaknesses.

1 _____

2 _____

# Activity 21 Red Cards

This is a difficult yet enjoyable task illustrating an interesting way in which you can act as facilitator *during* the group work.

Negotiation is multifarious in any organisation. In education it is crucial in many areas – from the setting of targets in appraisal to getting little Jo to come to school on time. Yet few people in education have any training in management.

Effective managerial negotiation (in its broadest sense) is about 'active listening': not presenting your own opinions first but seeking initially to understand the other person's view. It is about approaching problematic situations with a win/win philosophy, whereby we seek the best possible outcome for all parties concerned.

## Objective

To explore negotiating strategies

## Target group

All levels

*Group work* – groups of four to six

## Duration

One hour, 20 minutes

## Materials

One copy of Sheet 21.1 *Worksheet* for each group
One copy of Sheet 21.2 *Debrief* for each participant
One copy of *Key skills sheet 2* for each participant
Some red cards for you

## Operation

1 Divide participants into groups. Give each group a copy of the *Worksheet* (Sheet 21.1). Tell them that they have 20 minutes to complete the task BUT, if you catch them in an activity that is counter to good negotiating practice you will award them a red card. Three red cards and the group loses! Start the clock.

During the activity go round the groups and listen in to the discussions. Award red cards where you hear the argument getting heated and people interjecting rudely; and, especially, where you observe people so intent on presenting their own views that they are not listening to anyone else. Try not to let any group *quite* get the three red cards!

2 Stop the task after 20 minutes and take the participants through the debrief sheet to sift the five true statements from the false ones. Emphasise that the point of this is not to present hard and fast rules for negotiating practice but to promote discussion and exploration (in itself a model for the first stage in good negotiation!)
(*About 20 minutes*)

3 *Action task* Give everyone a copy of the *Debrief sheet* (Sheet 21.2) and a copy of *Key skills sheet* 2. Ask them, back in their groups, to select a subject on which they frequently negotiate in their role as managers (eg speaking to a parent about a difficult child and agreeing a course of action). Ask them to formulate a broad schema for such a negotiation, ie the stages they would like to lead the discussion through. Under each stage they should note the sort of questions to ask and the things to avoid.
(*30 minutes*)

4 Sum up the salient points and suggest they try to utilise a similar schematic approach to their negotiations with staff and others.

## In the classroom...

The *Red Card* game works well with young people, especially for the analysis of good group work. Give them a task and tell them they get the cards for bad group work practice. They quickly catch on and become, for example, wonderful listeners! You can play the game a number of times, each time looking out for a different element... positive questioning of one another, sensitivity etc. Give it a try!

I pride myself on being the kind of Head that listens to staff. It wasn't like that in my day as a probationary teacher... well times were different then, of course!... do you know, one day I was teaching Three Ackinson.. I think it was Three Ackinson, anyway, it had been a hell of a lesson, well it's like that when you're just starting out isn't it, anyway the bell was about to go, where was I? Oh yes... the bell was about to go and my Head... Crabtree... yes, good old Crabtree. Crab by name and Crab by nature, where was I? Oh yes... he came in... and believe you me... he was the sort of person who when he started you couldn't get a word in edgeways... know what I mean... anyway... where was I... Oh yes...

## Key skills sheet 2

# Worksheet

A substantial body of research indicates that FIVE of the following statements are true of top professional negotiators and FIVE are false.

As a team, decide by consensus the ones you feel are True.

1   They state their case clearly.
2   They are excellent listeners.
3   They use lots of arguments to support their case.
4   They never make comments on the way the other side is behaving during the negotiation.
5   They ask lots of questions.
6   They avoid the attack/defend spiral. (An escalating process where one side attacks the other and the other defends, then attacks back.)
7   They use terms like 'With respect 'or 'It's a very generous offer!'
8   They ask the other side 'Are they your only arguments?'
9   They tell the other side why their argument is wrong.
10  They answer questions with questions.

# Debrief sheet

By their very nature, good negotiation strategies vary according to the demands of the specific situation. The generalised statements below (linked to Key Skills Sheet 4) are designed to *promote discussion* and to unpack some general 'do's and 'don't's. They are *not* presented as hard and fast rules!

1      They state their case clearly.
FALSE *Leaving the opposition in doubt as to exactly what you want may strengthen your hand in negotiation. It is better to lead them around to your ideas... getting them to present your case for you!*

2      They are excellent listeners.
TRUE *It is important to understand the other's perspective. You can only do this by listening carefully to text and subtext of another's argument. To show the other person you are listening carefully is important in establishing trust and rapport.*

3      They use lots of arguments to support their case.
FALSE *Argument is not a pair of scales where ten on one side beats nine on the other. Using few but strong arguments is good negotiation practice.*

4      They never make comments on the way the other side is behaving during the negotiation.
FALSE *There are times when it is important to tell the other side honestly how you feel about them and the way they are conducting themselves.*

5      They ask lots of questions.
TRUE *By asking lots of questions you really understand the other side's point of view.*

6      They avoid the attack/defend spiral.
TRUE *Such extended exchanges are fruitless and entrench positions.*

7      They use terms like 'With respect' or 'It's a very generous offer!'
FALSE *Such ways of speaking put people's backs up and make them defensive.*
*('With respect...' usually means 'I don't in the least respect what you are saying!')*

8      They ask the other side 'Are they your only arguments?'
TRUE *This is a 'dirty trick' in negotiation... asked that question the opposition is likely to list other and weaker arguments which are easier to defeat!*

9 They tell the other side why their argument is wrong.
FALSE *Good practice is to lead the other side to explore for themselves the weaknesses of their position.*

10     They answer questions with questions.
TRUE *First, it helps you to give the impression of not being too intransigent in your demands. Second, it helps you to understand precisely the other side's intentions. Third, done sparingly and sensitively this technique helps to establish trust and rapport.*

# Activity 22 2,4,6

This is another activity on negotiation. It's an excellent demonstration piece on good argument practice, that you can use as a warm-up to any discussion-based task.

## Objective

To suggest good practice in discussion/argument

## Target group

All levels

*Whole group work* followed by small groups

## Duration

About one hour

## Materials

Flipchart
Pens and paper

## Operation

1 Assemble the group around the flipchart and write '2, 4, 6' on it. Explain the task:

*These three numbers are bound by a rule. By suggesting other numbers you may discover what the rule is. I'll tell you if the numbers you give me fit the rule.*

2 Take suggestions from the group and write them on the flipchart. The rule is 'any three numbers' so all initial suggestions will fit and it will take the group a long while to discover what the rule is.

Your purpose is to reflect upon the thinking processes behind the group's suggestions and to illustrate how they are relevant to the art of argument. (Any ideas? Before you read on, try this out on someone and see what numbers they suggest.)

3 Debrief...
● *Behind the suggestion '4, 6, 8' etc is thinking that goes 'I think the rule is that the numbers go up in twos. I'll give a suggestion to prove myself right.'* Here the solution precedes the enquiry, which then serves to justify it.

The same happens in bad argument/dicussion practice. People present their own counter-arguments to others, then spend their time supporting these (by making statements) rather than challenging the opponents' arguments (through asking questions).
● *Good scientific method would be to try to disprove the rule, ie 'I think the numbers go up in a progression of twos. Let me try to disprove this by suggesting, 1, 1, 1.'* Even quicker is a method of random thought: '11, 19, 602'.

In negotiation and effective group work, questioning ideas presented leads to discussion and exploration of possibilities. Presenting counter-propositions to these ideas leads to conflict and the creation of entrenched positions.

4 *Action task* Ask participants to get into small groups. Each member in turn presents a proposition for discussion. The others are only permitted to challenge by asking questions, not through presenting counter-proposals.

# Activity 23 Car Park

Another negotiation activity, which also illustrates a productive way of sub-dividing groups.

## Objective

To explore arbitration strategies

## Target group

All levels

*Groups of eight, initially sub-divided into pairs*

## Duration

About one hour

## Materials

Pens and paper

## Operation

1 Ask groups to divide into pairs and explain as follows:

*One pair wants to build a car park on a piece of waste ground near a housing estate.*
*The second pair wants to build a children's playground.*
*The third pair are arbitrators.*
*The fourth pair are to evalute how well the arbitrators perform their role.*

Allow about 15 minutes for the two sides to prepare their arguments, the arbitrators to plan their strategy and the evaluators to prepare criteria.

2 Bring the groups together to discuss the issue, with the evaluators observing the negotiation/arbitration.
(*Allow about 15 minutes*)

3 Ask the evaluators to report their findings. Invite the group to discuss these and define about six general points for effective arbitration.

4 Debrief some evaluation points...

1 *How well did the arbitrators solicit information? Did both parties feel they were asked questions equally and given equal time for explanation/presentation of their cases?*
2 *Did the arbitrators chair the discussion well? Did they keep the disputing parties on track?*
3 *Did they sequence the discussion effectively?*
4 *Did they request clarification enough/were they totally clear on both parties' arguments as presented?*
5 *Did they present compromise scenarios or did they perceive their role as deciding between the arguments of the disputing sides (the former, in most managerial situations is usually best!)*
6 *Did they sum-up well? Was their decision 'just'? Were reasons for it explained? Did both parties believe they had been handled fairly?*

**Key skills sheet 2**

# Activity 24 20 Questions

The following activity gets participants to analyse some practical indicators to the success of their management approaches and stimulates discussion on good practice.

## Objectives

To promote discussion on key leadership skills
To target specific areas for development

## Target groups

Senior and Middle Managers

*Solo work* followed by full-group discussion

## Duration

About one hour

## Materials

A copy of Sheet 24.1 *Questionnaire* and Sheet 21.2 *Debrief notes* for each participant
Pens

## Operation

1 Give each participant a copy of Sheet 24.1 *Questionnaire* and ask them to answer the questions. Tell them that no-one will see what they have written. (You could, if you prefer, read out the questions one after the other, allowing time for completion. Or, to save time and allow a more considered response, you might give out the questionnaire prior to your session and ask participants to fill it in before they come.)
Wait for everyone to finish: usually about 15 minutes.

2 Bring the group together in a circle and give out the *Debrief notes* (Sheet 24.2). Take them through the notes sequentially, discussing the statements made about good leadership practice.
(*About 30 minutes*)

3 *Action task* Ask participants to look again at their questionnaire answers together with the *Debrief notes*. Invite them to target one area for improvement in their own leadership style.
(*Allow about ten minutes*)

4 Get each in turn to report on their developmental target. Discuss as a whole group the *practical* steps each person might take to achieve their desired improvement.
(*20 to 30 minutes depending upon size of the group*)

5 Suggest they do it!

## Key skills sheets 2 and 5

# Questionnaire

Answer the questions in the space provided.
('Team' refers to the people you have responsibility for managing.)

1    When was the last time you stated your personal working objectives to your team or produced a 'mission' or developmental statement for their consultation?

_____

2    When was the last time you consulted with a member of your team prior to reaching a decision?

_____

3    State three tasks that you have delegated to individual team members within the last three months...
(i) _____
(ii) _____
(iii) _____

4    State a 'non-negotiable' or a 'bottom-line' issue where you and you alone retain the right of decision...

_____

5    When was the last time you researched or read in depth about an educational issue?

_____

6    Name the last book you read on management.

_____

7    What is the next management problem you have to deal with?

_____

8    When was the last time you compromised with someone to solve a problem? _____

9    Have you been approached recently by a team member wishing to speak to you about another team member?

_____

10    Write down the name of someone you praised within the last seven days.

_____

11    Write down the name of someone you criticised recently.

_____

12    Did you criticise them to their face or behind their back?

_____

13    Who came to you to share a problem recently?

_____

14    Who came to you to share a success recently?

_____

15    Write down the name of one of your team followed by a developmental target you have for them.

_____

16    Do you treat everyone in your team the same?

_____

17    What's second on your list of developmental priorities for your team?

_____

18    When do you intend to start work on the above priority?

_____

19    What has been your team's most recent success?

_____

20    Are you liked by most people?

_____

# Debrief notes

The following notes relate each question asked to a statement on good practice for your discussion...

1  It is important for a manager to clearly define and express their objectives and motives to their subordinates. It facilitates working towards 'shared objectives'. Different perceptions need to be talked through and consensus reached.

2  Consultation is extremely important to team building, sustaining and developing motivation and inculcating a sense of 'ownership'.

3  Delegation is an important tool of management for logistical *and* staff development reasons. Each person should know their function within the team and have their individual role to fulfil.

4  A manager should define and communicate their non-negotiables. Subordinates will know what is expected of them and what areas of responsibility are the sole preserve of their manager.

5  A manager needs theoretical as well as practical expertise for their team to draw upon and, of course, needs to keep in touch with new developments.

6  For a manager in education it is just as important to develop expertise in people management as it is in curriculum management. There are many excellent books on the subject!

7  Effective management is about being proactive: anticipating and mitigating potential difficulties.

8  Managers need to develop a win/win approach to management problems. All issues other than pre-defined non-negotiables should be *really* negotiable.

9  People need to feel that they can trust their managers and that confidentiality will be respected.

10  As well as knowing that they are doing a good job, people need to be *told* it! People who feel good about themselves produce good results. Giving praise where it is due is arguably the most important ingredient in the effective management of people.
Make a point of thanking people.

11  Constructive and sensitive criticism based upon mutual respect and trust is fundamental to staff development. People should always be clear that it is not *them* you are criticising but their action or specific failing. In reprimanding, always separate the person from their mistake and *end* on a positive reinforcement of their qualities. Criticism on its own is not enough, it must always be accompanied by the contracting of support in rectifying the problem.

12  As a manager you need to establish an atmosphere whereby you can always be open with people, face to face, about the problems you have with their work/attitude.

13  People need to feel that they can share all their professional problems with you and that you might be of some help to them. Let them know of your willingness to listen and ask them periodically if they have any problems.

14  Sharing successes is just as important as sharing problems – if not more so. People gain prestige and build their confidence through such a process. Managers should openly solicit such sharing.

15   Managers should know the strengths and weaknesses of their subordinates, so they may build upon the former and help to rectify the latter. A clear, negotiated, and supported programme of individual staff  development should always be 'on-going'.

16   Managers need to apply 'different strokes to different folks'. Each team member should be treated according to their individual needs and requirements.

17   Managers need to negotiate and set short, medium- and long-term developmental targets for their teams. Change is an important dynamic in the vitality of an organisation. People need to know 'where they are going'.

18   Effective development requires giving careful consideration to the timescale.

19   Managers need to set themselves realistic criteria for success. People need to know that they are achieving results.

20   What we tend to like most about people is their honesty, sensitivity and openness in their dealings with us. This is the bedrock of good management.

# Activity 25 Trouble Shooting...
# and the Management of Conflict

Management theories look fine on paper, but what about in practice when we are dealing with real people in often difficult situations?

This activity uses the debrief sheet from Activity 24 *20 Questions* as a stimulus to explore 'real' problems faced by managers in the practical application of theory. In doing so, it simultaneously reinforces the pointers to good practice! This can make a good follow-up session to the previous activity.

## Objectives

To discuss real managerial problems within the organisation
To explore remedies to these problems

## Target groups

Senior and Middle Managers

*Small groups* of four ideally

## Duration

One hour, 15 minutes

## Materials

A copy of Sheet 24.2 *Debrief sheet* (from the previous activity) for each participant
Flip chart
Pens

## Operation

1 Divide participants into groups and ask them to sit in circles.

2 Give out copies of the *Debrief sheet* and take them through the points. Ask them to make comments as you proceed. Make a note of any 'buts' or problems presented to you on a flip chart. Don't discuss the points raised at this stage, merely accept them.
(*No more than 15 minutes*)

3 Set the following task:
*As a group, study the theoretical points on the sheet. Share individual management problems that you have encountered or are encountering in attempting to fulfil the good practice expounded here. For example, you might agree that good practice is being sensitive to the needs of your staff; but what about when the needs of one of your staff seem to be at odds with the general good of everyone else?*
Make a note of the problems thus raised on your flipchart.
(*Allow about 15 minutes*)

4 Ask the group to select from the list of problems one that is current and pressing for one of the group. The idea is to approach the problem coldly and analytically. Invite the group to consider the following questions:
(You could have noted these on a page of the flip chart prior to the session.)
1 *Precisely define the nature of the problem. Is it a two-way problem between the manager and subordinate with both parties equally to blame? Or is one or the other more/totally to blame?*
2 *Is it a problem that can be left to sort itself out/ blow over? Or does action need to be taken?*
3 *If action needs to be taken, is it action the Manager should take or should it be 'delegated' upwards – ie support requested from a more Senior colleague. If so, what can they do that you can't?*
4 *If the manager needs/wants to deal with the problem, what possible courses of action are open*

to them? *Discuss possibilities and decide on the best one.* Ask them to make detailed notes during the discussion.
(*Allow 30 minutes*)

5 Get the groups to share the problems they have discussed and their strategies for dealing with them.

6 *Action task* Sharing and discussion of individual managerial problems can provide much-needed support. Ask people to think about ways they can offer each other time to air these and other problems, confidentially, in future Middle Management or Senior Management meetings. Perhaps there could be a formal structure for sharing individual problems at, say, three-monthly intervals?

**Key skills sheet 4**

# Section Three: Working together in appraisal

# Activity 26 The Structured Brainstorm

A positive system of staff appraisal is of enormous benefit to any organisation. If the element of perceived threat is removed, the appraisal can be seen as a process for sharing successes, highlighting the employee's needs and negotiating consensus on developmental targets. It becomes a win/win process for both the individual teacher and the school itself.

This and the following activity are designed as a 'cascade'. You run the activities with Senior Management first; they then run them with the HoDs, who in turn run them with their teams. (You can, of course, photocopy the instructions to give out after your workshop.) The outcomes of each workshop in the 'cascade' should be summarised, written up and presented to all staff for further comments. Ideally, all the material should then go to a representative staff committee who will draw up guidelines for Staff Appraisal. As a result, you will have an appraisal system that is your own – one that complies with legal requirements but is potentially more significant to the ethos and sucess of your school.

The activity also highlights some useful training strategies that are readily adaptable to other themes. These are pointed out in the notes. The structure of the session progressively builds focus and achieves excellent results in a short period of time. It's best to cascade the whole process, so that all the groups are enabled to share their opinions in an equally productive way.

## Objectives

To share opinions on appraisal
To facilitate staff involvement in setting up an appraisal system

## Target group

Senior Management to cascade

*Small groups* (divide into groups of four if working with a large Senior Management Team)

## Duration

About one hour, 15 minutes

## Materials

Pens and paper

## Operation

1 Ask the group to sit in circles of four. Explain the 'Structured Brainstorm Technique':
*The brainstorm method has two rules:*
1 *Each person around the circle contributes in turn.*
2 *No argument is allowed. The ideas are all accepted by the group without comment.*
(Here is the first useful training device... it gets everyone to contribute equally and without fear of having their views put down by someone else – a factor that all-too-frequently inhibits contributions.)

2 Begin with an idea to help the groups practise the brainstorm technique, for example:
*What would happen if gravity stopped for a minute each and every day? Make suggestions in turn around the group and remember... no arguing allowed!*
(Training device two: get the participants to play with ideas in a fun way first, prior to tackling the issues themselves. This helps to generate a more thought-out and creative response later. Maxim... practise skills before using them!)
(*Five minutes*)

3 Next give the groups a negative proposition to try out (still a step away from the theme):
*Go round the group in turn and say what you feel Education should NOT be about!*
(This is device three, using the negative to spark the positive. We frequently find it easier to explain what something shouldn't be than to explain what it should be! The inferences in the negative contributions tend to sharpen the positive statements that you will ask for later.)
(*Five minutes*)

69

4 Give the group a sheet of paper and ask them to brainstorm what an appraisal system should *not* be about. There is no need to stick to the round circle structure any more, but emphasise that getting down a number of statements at this stage is more important than arguing about their validity.
(*About 15 minutes*)

5 Ask the group now to word a number of positive statements defining the objectives of appraisal. They can use their negatives as a starting-point:
'In order that (negative statement)... an appraisal system should (positive statement).'
eg 'In order that it should not be seen as the sole preserve of senior management, an appraisal system should include all teachers in the school.'
(*About 30 minutes*)

6 Share the statements (or they could be typed up for sharing later). Debrief the processes used to arrive at them.
(*Ten minutes*)

7 *Action task* Suggest they use the structured brainstorm technique and the negative proposition method as tools for their team work. The former is useful when discussion gets 'bogged-down'; the latter is a useful device in anticipating potential problems involved in new initiatives.

## In the classroom...

A similar sequential building process can be applied to discussion work in a variety of classroom situations. Importantly, it develops concentration and involvement.

**Key skills sheets 10 and 8**

# Activity 27 Pros, Cons and Interesting Points Analysis

Say you are going to set up a broad Appraisal System for the reasons outlined in the introduction to Activity 26. Who appraises whom? A HoD, for example, could be appraised by a Senior Manager, by another HoD, by a member of their team or the whole of their department together. They could even appraise themselves!

My second cascade system gets staff to explore the possible options along with their benefits and disadvantages. Should you wish to 'install' a particular predetermined appraisal system, you will find the exercise below useful for facilitating detailed discussion upon its advantages and suggestions for overcoming its problems. Indeed, the 'Pros, Cons and Interesting Points' ideas analysis system, as described, has a variety of uses. It's an excellent method for brainstorming and analysing ideas. Again the idea is for Senior Managers to cascade the workshop/method through their departments/staff.

## Objectives

To analyse possible appraisal systems
To illustrate an adaptable method of ideas analysis

## Target group

Senior Management to cascade

*Small groups* – divide into groups of three if working with a large team

## Duration

One hour, 35 minutes

## Materials

A copy of Sheet 27.1 *Pros, cons and interesting points* for each group.

## Operation

1 Ask the participants to sit in a small circle or circles.

2 Teach the 'Pros, Cons and Interesting Points' discussion method:
*Label yourselves in turn around the group... 'Pro' or 'Con' or 'Interesting'* (Larger groups repeat the labels in sequence). *If you are a 'Pro' person you must argue for the proposition that's presented to you, regardless of personal opinions on the subject. If you are a 'Con' you must argue against the proposition presented. If you are an 'Interesting' person you are group entertainer! You come down on neither one side nor the other of the argument, you merely reflect upon it. When you have been round the group once, swap roles and argue in your new role on the same issue. Go round three times, so each person gets a chance to argue from a different perspective.*

3 Using the above method, get the group to argue 'Pro', 'Con', or 'Interesting' on the following proposition...
*It would be better to live your life backwards, beginning at the age of 80 and getting gradually younger till you ended up in the womb!*
This offers a fun way of practising skills prior to using them.
(It usually takes about ten minutes to complete the three rounds of the above.)

4 Give the group a copy of Sheet 27.1. Instruct them as follows:
*In the 'Possibles' column, list six variations you can think of for an appraisal system (you could give a couple of examples from the introduction). Do not at this stage discuss them, just list them. You have 15 minutes.*
Discussion normally breaks out too early in the ideas development process. Arguing over possibilities one and two means that potentially better ones don't even get thought of! This simple method allows the ideas to come first, examination later. Again, it is very adaptable and you'll find that ideas that come last are frequently the best ones.

5  Ask the group to go through the possibilities and put an asterisk by the ones that look most feasible. (*Ten minutes*)

6  Now get them to use the 'Pros', 'Cons' and 'Interesting points' columns to analyse each asterisked idea in turn; ie looking at what's for the system, what's against it, what's interesting about it. By the end of this, one of the systems is likely to look the best. It will have a lot of Pros, a few Cons and a number of Interesting points (these are likely to be things that give an idea that additional spark that helps to make it a winner).
(*Allow about 30 minutes for this section.*)

7  Invite the group to find the favourite system and focus on the points raised in the Cons section to develop improvements:
*For each Con against the favoured system, devise an improvement to mitigate it. Note this in the 'CS' section of the Con box – this stands for 'Counter Strategies'.*

8  Debrief the processes you've taken the group through. Type up the favoured system or systems selected, together with their 'Pros, Cons, Counter Strategies and Interesting Points'.

9  *Action task* Suggest that the participants use the 'Pros, Cons and Interesting Points' analysis as a teamwork tool in their action planning. It's especially useful when consensus is difficult to achieve.

## In the classroom...

The 'Pros, Cons and Interesting Points' method of argument and its round-group structure is useful for young people as a precursor to discussion work. It helps to elicit contributions from everyone.

**Key skills sheets 10 and 11**

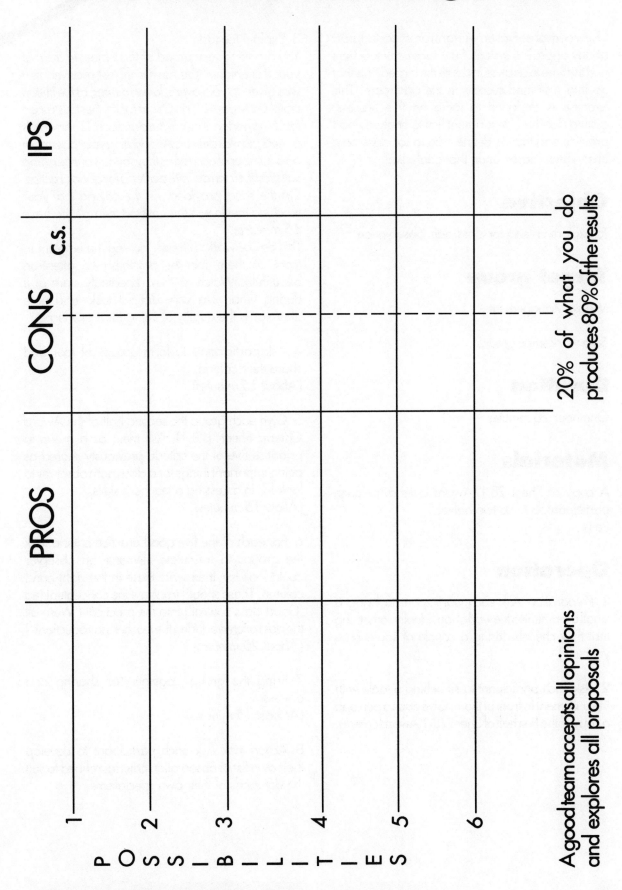

# Activity 28 Oscars

Classroom observation will form an important part of any appraisal system. Few successful teachers find the time to analyse in depth the ingredients that go into sustained success in the classroom. This exercise is designed to focus on this process; getting Heads of Department first to analyse good practice and then to define criteria for classroom observation based upon that analysis.

## Objective

To explore criteria for classroom observation

## Target group

Middle Management

*Solo work* small groups

## Duration

One hour 20 minutes

## Materials

A copy of Sheet 28.1 *Award criteria* for each participant, cut into two halves
Pens

## Operation

1 *Preparation* Ask each participant to bring a small ornament to the workshop, ideally something that they cherish! (Bring a couple of spare ones yourself.)

2 Ask each participant to sit behind a table with the ornament in front of them. Give each a pen and a copy of the first half of Sheet 28.1 *Award criteria*.

3 Explain the task:
*You are very, very proud of this object in front of you. It is unique. You have only just received it. It was given to you, over a lavish dinner, at the Hilton Hotel in London. It is an Oscar for the best sustained teaching performance in the classroom! The awards panel's job was difficult. After visiting your classroom on a number of occasions they found your teaching satisfied their ten definitive criteria for good practice. On the sheet provided, list the criteria that your teaching met to win this coveted award! You have 15 minutes.*

This device works a treat! Having the emblem in front of them focuses participants' attention beautifully. Watch as they repeatedly stare at it during what is a very difficult task, and note afterwards the quality of the ideas it produces!

4 Ask participants to form groups of four and share their criteria.
(*About 15 minutes*)

5 Give each group the second half of the *Award Criteria Sheet* (28.1). Ask them *as a group* to prioritise five of the criteria previously shared as being important things for a classroom observer to look for in assessing a teacher's skills.
(*Allow 15 minutes*)

6 For each of the five good practice criteria, ask the groups to formulate elements an observer could look for, then write these in the right-hand column. These should translate the conceptual (eg 'Good class control') into the practical ('Were all the class attentive during the teacher's introduction?')
(*About 20 minutes*)

7 Bring the groups together for sharing and discussion.
(*At least 15 minutes*)

8 *Action task* Ask each participant to develop their own list of observation criteria, refined to suit the demands of their own specialisms.

## In the classroom...

I've used the Oscar game to very good effect with young people. I've told them that they've received their Oscar for their own qualities as a person, asked them to list these attributes and used this as a basis for discussing the importance of building self-esteem. Perhaps you can think of some other ways to use the idea?

**Key skills sheet 11**

## Award Criteria

Criteria for first-rate classroom practice

1 _____

2 _____

3 _____

4 _____

5 _____

6 _____

7 _____

8 _____

9 _____

10 _____

-------------------------------------------- ✂

**Selected criteria**

Write in this column....

1

2

3

4

5

# Activity 29 Action Planning

I include this activity here, linked into the theme of appraisal, although its application is a wide one. It leads participants through a step-by-step structure for developmental planning.

## Objectives

To illustrate a method for developmental action planning
To apply this method to setting up an appraisal system

## Target group

Senior Management, although both the exercises and the central tasks can be used with a variety of groups

*Small groups* – I'll assume for what follows a small Senior Team of four members. For larger groups, divide into fours first.

## Duration

For best results, about two hours, 45 minutes for the entire workshop.

## Materials

A copy of Sheet 29.1 *Task* for each group
A copy of *Key skills sheet 8 Action Planning* for each participant
Pens and paper

## Operation

1 Seat the group in a small circle. Explain that, without introduction, you are going to give them a task and that you'll fully debrief it afterwards. The ground-rule for the task is that they may not move from their seats to try out anything. They will be given ten minutes to talk the task over and plans its successful operation; then, upon instruction, they will have just one minute to complete the task. There are hidden problems that will need solving!

2 Give them a copy of Sheet 29.1 *Task* and get them going.
(*Allow ten minutes*)

3 Stop the planning process and ask them to complete the task in one minute.

4 Debrief :
*The task itself was a metaphor for the developmental planning process as follows...*
(1) *Successful completion required first and foremost a close visualisation of the outcome. Effective developmental planning requires such a vision.*
(2) *Given a vision of the outcome, you then needed to work BACKWARDS to achieve the result. This 'backwards' thinking is an important part of developmental planning. Primarily it allows one to be pro-active...As in the game, it allows you to anticipate problems prior to their occurrence and adjust your planning accordingly.*
(3) *Given a vision of the end result and a backwards thinking process, you could then clearly define each person's role in achieving the desired outcome. You finally gave each member of the team a different task.*

5 Explain that you are now going to apply this process to the planning of an appraisal system.

6 Give out pens and paper and ask the participants to write a description of the system they wish to develop at the school, by completing clearly and concisely the following statements:
• *Our appraisal system will consist of...*
• *It will serve the purpose of....*
(*Allow 20 minutes or so*)

7 They have their vision. Ask them now to set a time-scale: *Let's assume it's Spring and you want your appraisal system up and running by next September. That should be a reasonable time to get things right!*

8 Give each participant a copy of Key skills sheet 8 *Action planning.* Ask them to separate for ten minutes and individually complete the left-hand column of Section two, entitled: 'Probable problems in achieving development'.

Separating the members of a group like this, at this time in the process, is a productive way of working. Working individually they are likely to focus on different areas; presenting a broader overview when they combine their ideas later.

9 Get the group to share their thoughts on the possible problems to be countered. Ask them, as a group, to complete the 'Countered by...' column in Section two. These are the proactive measures they will take to ensure that the problems will not arise.
(*30 minutes*)

10 Ask groups to fill in Section three A by breaking down the countering tactics from Section two into a number of clearly-defined tasks.
(*20 minutes*)

11 In Section three B, ask them to define the other tasks they feel need to be done to achieve their desired outcome. These will tend to be bureaucratic, logistical and training objectives: for example, writing and publishing guidelines on the appraisal process, allowing for staff consultation procedures, training appraisers/appraisees etc.
(*20 minutes*)

12 In the timescale column of Section three, ask them to set deadlines for the completion of each of the tasks.
(*Ten minutes or so*)

13 Refer them to Section four and ask them to complete it as follows:
*Now divide the tasks among the individual team members as indicated. Fill in the NAME of the team member. Next to 'TO' write a brief task definition, to clarify your function within the team. Next to 'FOR' write your statement of purpose, so that your work has clearly-defined intentions. 'HOW' means your method of working, so you need to analyse the most effective way of completing your task. Next to 'BY' write the deadline you agreed earlier. For 'CRITERIA FOR SUCCESS' think about how you will evaluate how successfully you have completed the task. Working towards these criteria will help to 'centre' your activities for the desired outcomes.*

14 Finally, get the group to use the time-scale in Section five to plan a suitable number of report-back and evaluation meetings prior to their deadline. This requires cross-reference on individual task deadlines and allowance for course changes in response to the inevitable unforeseen problems!
(*15 minutes*)

15 Discuss the efficacy of the system you've been demonstrating and other applications of the process.

16 *Action task* Suggest that each team member adopt this method for a trial period on a development they are facilitating with other staff.

**Key skills sheet 8**

## Task

In ten minutes time you will be asked to reposition your chairs and sit on them so that...

1    No two team members are facing the same way.
2    Not everyone is seated with arms folded.
3    Not everyone is seated without arms folded.
4    Not everyone has crossed legs.
5    Not everyone has uncrossed legs.
6    No one with crossed legs has arms folded.
7    No one with uncrossed legs has arms unfolded.

No 'rehearsal' is allowed. You must prepare for the operation purely by discussion.

# Activity 30 Setting Up Role Plays... in general, and in appraisal interview training

Role play can be a highly productive training tool. However, many trainers find it a difficult method to use and many teachers are wary of engaging in the activity. The following is a step-by-step guide to 'warming' participants into role play work. I've taken Training for Appraisal as a suitable theme although the methodology may be applied to any use of role play. On Sheet 30.1 I've noted WHY I apply the processes I do. I hope you will find this useful in planning other role play sessions. Follow the system in sequence, whatever your training theme, and you won't go far wrong in using role play to good and enjoyable effect!

*The appraisal interview...*
For appraisal to be of maximum benefit it needs to become part of the culture of a school; not just the preserve of the responsible Senior Teacher. To this end, HoDs should be encouraged to use appraisal positively as part of their own management processes, perhaps a once-yearly appraisal interview with each of their department could form a part of this. Both the appraisers and the appraisees need to receive some training to derive benefit...

## Objectives

To develop a technique for using role play
To give participants practice in appraisal interviewing techniques

## Target groups

Heads of department and other appraisers....

*Pair work*

## Duration

About one and a half hours

## Materials

A copy of *Key skills sheet 10* for each participant.
Pens and paper
(A large enough room for your group to work comfortably with space between each pair.)
You might also like to give each participant a copy of Sheet 30.1 for use with their departments.

## Operation

1 Ask the participants to find a partner and sit with them away from other pairs.

2 Ask pairs to arrange their two chairs in a position most comfortable for one-to-one communication. Get them to experiment with the chair positions, distances apart etc for a couple of minutes. Debrief:
*The best position for the two chairs is at a 90° angle. Why? It establishes neutral space between the two people, allowing them to disengage eye-contact while talking (we do this naturally, it seems to aid our thinking). It also places interviewer and interviewee on an equal footing. Face-to-face is far less comfortable. In the appraisal interview, a coffee table in front of the two chairs, where each may put down their notes, helps to establish the 'safety' of the space. Never conduct the interview across a desk! It presents a psychological barrier as well as a physical one.*

3 Get pairs to play a short concentration game. Adding games are ideal. For example (and fitting the theme): one partner says a single word that might describe people's feelings towards an appraisal interview, the other repeats that word and adds another. The first person repeats both words and adds a third and so on.
(*About five minutes*)

4 Ask partners to label themselves either A or B. Explain how you are going to work...

*I am going to take all the As out of the room and tell them something I am not going to tell the Bs. When I return I will give the Bs a task.*

*Whilst doing the task they have to try and work out what I told the As to do! The Bs can stop the task as soon as they've discovered what the As are up to.*

5 Ask the As to leave the room with you and explain their role...

*I'm going to ask your partner 'B' to talk to you about their professional strengths for a couple of minutes. Each time they say 'Er' or 'Um' or 'You know' etc. I want you to count out loud: 'One, two, three and so on!'*

Take the As back in. Tell the Bs to talk about their strengths whilst trying to guess what their partner is doing. (*Stop the activity after about five minutes*).

6 Debrief the last task (it's connected with appraisal!)...

*The Bs probably found it difficult to speak about their strengths. We seem to find it easier to be self-critical than to be positive about ourselves. Getting the appraisee to be positive about themselves is an important part of the appraiser's role in the interview. An appraiser should focus initially on the appraisee's strengths, not their weaknesses.*

*In order to fulfil their role the As had to listen intently to the Bs... an obvious parallel to appraisal. The appraiser also needs to be sensitive to the underlying feelings behind what is being said. This way they can pick up upon inferences of subtext to ask the subsidiary questions that open up a real dialogue.*

7 *Take the Bs outside. Tell them that this time the As will talk about their strengths. Meanwhile the Bs are to 'posturally echo' their partner: sitting and gesticulating in exactly the same way! Bring the Bs back and instruct the As to talk about their strengths.* (*Five minutes*)

8 Debrief the task...

*Postural echo (in its less extreme forms!) is a useful aid in establishing a rapport with people. Salespeople are taught to posturally echo potential clients for this reason! At the start of the appraisal interview, if the appraiser sits in a similar way to the appraisee, believe it or not, it will help to ease both into conversation.*

9 Take the As outside again and explain as follows:

*B is an old friend whom you are meeting again in a pub after a long separation. You are desperate to find out all about what they've been up to recently.*

Ask the As to stay outside the door for a moment whilst you tell the Bs something you don't want them to hear! Give the Bs their role...

*A is an old friend whom you are meeting again in a pub after a long separation. You are meeting them just out of politeness. You don't really like them. You think they are far too nosey!*

Let the As in and allow five minutes or so for the role play.

10 Debrief, focusing on the importance of questioning skills to the appraiser, and of sensitivity towards how the questions are being received and responded to.

11 Give each participant a copy of *Key skills sheet 10*. Briefly take them through the interview structure. Ask each to select a section of the plan (a different one from their partner). Ask them to leave their partner for a little while and on a sheet of paper jot down a few suitable questions they could use as an appraiser to facilitate the desired responses from their appraisee.
(*Ten minutes*)

12 Bring the pairs back together again and ask them to take turns to be appraiser and appraisee. They have ten minutes for each role. The appraiser should use the questions they have just devised. Add an element of difficulty (and conflict) to the role play by telling them that as appraisee they should be a little reluctant in answering. Hence the appraiser, as frequently in the real situation, will need to ask subsidiary questions to draw their partner out.
(*20 minutes in all*)

13 Debrief the significance of preparing focused questions for an appraisal interview and pre-thinking likely subsidiary questions.

14 *Action task...* Ask each person to select one of their own department members as a model and, with the help of their partner, draw up a questioning plan based around the Key Skills Sheet Structure.
(*30 minutes*)

**Key skills sheets 9 and 10**

# Notes on the role play methodology

1 (Step 2) Experimenting with the chairs is a mild 'physical' warm-up activity that is an important precursor to role play work. Language comes best through action.

2 (Step 3) Using an exercise like the 'adding game' is an important second step to leading your group into role play. It's an easy task with a clear structure to it. It breaks the ice, and, since it is a game, they are also beginning to 'play' without realising it; to let go a little of the some of the inhibitions that present themselves during in-role work.

3 (Step 4) The action of walking into the room helps to get things going. To start role plays it is often a good idea for one of the partners to physically enter the scene. ('Action first' again.) The challenge element of the exercise is also important. There's an incentive in finding the secret, which has a 'dispersal' function. It helps to unblock them during the role play task itself.

4 (Step 5) First, this kind of activity further breaks the ice and gets the fun going! Secondly, especially for the 'A's, it 'centres' the activity. (Centering, in actor's parlance, is the skill of making all exchanges flow from a central focus, their 'character'.) Giving participants a tight role play brief is an all-important first step to setting broader tasks. It helps build people's confidence and encourages them to develop role play skills prior to using them. It's a great mistake to go straight into open-ended verbal improvisations. Give them crutches to lean upon first and then progressively take them away...)

5 (Step 6) Detailed debrief is especially important after role play work. The participants need to know why they are doing what might appear otherwise to be just a silly game.

6 (Step 7) The 'B's now practise the concentration skills needed in 'centering'.

7 (Step 9) This gives further practice in asking questions, but you are now adding the ingredient of conflict. Conflict, in its broadest sense, is the proverbial basis of drama and the root of effective role play work. In any exchange between people there is an element of conflict (if only the edge of uncertainty provided by never quite knowing how someone will receive what you are saying.) In the above, and in all role play, the conflict provided by giving the participants differing briefs develops the flow of dialogue. Closely define both people's roles in the scene and make them different ones. It's even better if neither knows the other's role in the exchange. It adds reality! (PS Be sure to stop these activities early, just as they are beginning to enjoy themselves! It leaves them wanting more.)

8 The above process takes about 20 minutes. It is appropriate as a warm-up to any training theme where you are going to use role play effectively. Your participants will now feel much more confident and secure in their own role play abilities and will be enjoying the experience.

# Activity 31 Sensitive handling

Here's another way of using the same sequence and method of role play, on a different theme.

## Objective

To use role play to explore difficult one-to-one situations with staff

## Target group

Middle Management

*Pair work*

## Duration

About one hour

## Materials

Sheet 31.1 *Role pairs,* cut up – one role per participant
Paper and pens

## Operation

1 *Warm up* Divide the group into pairs with a chair for each participant. Explain

*I'm going to call out some different sorts of relationships. When I do, place the chairs in the formation you think best symbolises that relationship. OK?... affection! ... hostility!... embarrassment!*

2 *Concentration* Continue:
*Sit on the chairs, facing one-another. Look each other straight between the eyes. Hold that position for two minutes without smiling!*

3 Ask pairs to divide into 'A' and 'B'. Take the 'A's out of the room. Explain that they are going to practise persuasion skills.
*Your task is to try and persuade B that what they most need in life is a mobile telephone. However, at no time may you present the idea to them. You have to ask them questions that lead them into*

*saying that a mobile phone would be useful. You achieve your task when your partner presents the idea first.*

4 Take the 'A's back in and give them time to play the scene.

5 Take the 'B's out and explain:
*Your partner is a mean person. You want to borrow £100. If you asked for it directly they would say no. Find ways of getting them to volunteer the loan.*

6 Take the 'B's back in to play the scene.

7 Give out the role play briefs on the top half of Sheet 31.1. Give 'A's part A and 'B's part B. Make sure neither sees their partner's half.
(*Five minutes*)

8 Give out the role play briefs on the bottom half of Sheet 31.1, giving the 'B's part C and the 'A's part D.
(*Five minutes*)

9 Give each pair a sheet of paper and a pen. Ask them to devise a sequence of questions they might ask of an appraisee to draw from them an open expression of their problems.
(*Allow about 15 minutes*)

10 Bring everyone together to share their sequences of questions. Extract some general pointers, for example: how important it is initially to build up the appraisee's confidence and trust; how important it is to phrase the questions in such a way as to sustain focus without limiting their responses; how the sequence might take the appraisee from a general analysis into specifics.

11 Discuss how the participants might train their own departments in taking active roles as appraisees.

12 *Action task* Ask participants to evaluate the problems they feel exist for individual members of their departments. Suggest they begin addressing these issues through one-to-one meetings with their team.

# Role play in the classroom...

Use exactly the same 'stepping' process in using role plays with young people. Younger children find it very easy to go straight into role play: 'A' is parent, 'B 'is child. ..go! is frequently all it takes.

**Key skills sheets 2 and 10**

# Role Pairs

Role Play/Brief One

**A**  You are a Probationary Teacher having trouble controlling 9–Z during your English classes. You are embarrassed by this and don't wish to admit you need help.
Your partner is your Head of Department.

- - - - - - - - - - - - - - - - - - - - - - - - - - - - - - - - - - - - - ✂

**B**  You are Head of English. Your partner is a Probationary Teacher who shows great promise but has problems with 9-Z. You've passed the classroom and found the kids all over the place and being very noisy. You want to offer support in handling this class.

- - - - - - - - - - - - - - - - - - - - - - - - - - - - - - - - - - - - - ✂

Role Play/Brief Two

**C**  You are Second in the English Department. You have a family and are trying to sell your house to buy a more suitable, larger one. It's been on the market for a long time and you've just lost the one you wanted to buy. You know you've been pretty grumpy lately with the children and with your colleagues. But you know it's only temporary and feel that you can keep personal and professional problems separate. Your partner is your Head of Department.

- - - - - - - - - - - - - - - - - - - - - - - - - - - - - - - - - - - - - ✂

**D**  You are Head of English, your partner is Second in Department. Normally a very efficient and useful member of your team, recently they have been reluctant to stay after school for meetings and late in fulfilling their assigned tasks. You have also noticed a deterioration in their classroom work. Something is wrong and you want to contract support.

# Activity 32 Supporting

This activity illustrates another adaptable method for facilitating role play. Here it is related to training for the appraisal interview.

Appraisal is about providing support. The appraisal interview is just one part of an appraisal system. Whether formal or informal, such 'staff development' interviews (or 'evaluation meetings') should ideally be an on-going part of a manager's job: part of the support they provide. Many managers in education are wary of such meetings. This exercise, again, is useful practice...

## Objectives

To train appraisers and appraisees in reaching consensus

## Target groups

Heads of Department and other appraisers

*Pair work*

## Duration

About one and a half hours

## Materials

A copy of Sheet 32.1 *Role play brief*, on card and cut as indicated for each pair
Pens and paper

## Operation

1 Invite the groups to divide into pairs. Run the warm-up as described in the previous activity.
(*About 20 minutes*)

2 Give each of the partners a different role play card from Sheet 32.1. Instruct them not to show it to their partner. Give them time to prepare their strategy as noted on the card.
(*About ten minutes*)

3 Start the role play by asking the appraiser to sit down and the appraisee to enter the scene, then to act out the interview.
(*Allow about ten minutes for the role play*)

4 Stop the role play. Ask the partners to show one-another their role play cards. Give each pair a sheet of paper. Ask them to divide the sheet into two columns: 'effectual' and 'ineffectual':
*Under each column think about what you have just experienced in the role play. Note down in the appropriate column the communication strategies which seemed to work and those which didn't seem to work.*
(*Allow ten minutes*)

5 Bring the whole group together and debrief using a flip chart. You will find that the experience of the role play and its analysis has produced some useful interpersonal communication guidelines for reaching consensus. Debrief also the significance of 'fall-back' positions to the negotiation process, ie compromises you would be willing to accept.
(*About 20 minutes*)

6 *Action task* Working with their partner again, ask them to select one of their department members as a model for appraisal interview preparation. Ask them to do the following:
• *List the likely problems you would face as appraisers with this person.*
• *List the outcomes you would ideally like from the interview with this person.*
• *From the above, devise a list of 'fall-back' positions, ie the outcomes you would be prepared to accept should the ideal ones be unobtainable!*
(*About 20 minutes*)

*Notes on the role play method...*
The briefs given on the role play cards are obviously important to how well the interaction works. Here are a few guidelines on writing these cards:
1   Describe the character simply, using easily recognisable 'types'... in the example here I have used 'Moaner' and 'Arguer'.

2   Describe their function in the scene, ie something they are out to achieve. Give each character a different function.
3   Give them a way into the scene itself. Here, I've suggested a dialogue to get the ball rolling.

## Using role play in the classroom...

Use role play cards in exactly the same way. Select the scenarios for relevance to your pupils. Always allow a little time for the characters to prepare their roles. You could encourage pairs to show their work to the rest of the class for follow-up analysis. This method is especially useful in PSE for the exploration of alternative responses in conflict situations.

**Key skills sheets 2 and 10**

# Role play brief

## Appraiser

You are Head of a large department.

You are inclined to be a bit of an 'arguer', tending to confront people abrasively. You realise you need to watch this tendency as it can be counter-productive.

Your appraisee is a colleague who has been in teaching a long time and is very traditional in their methods. These are frequently inappropriate to the kind of children in your school.

You would like to get the appraisee to undertake some training in Active Learning. You know of a course available. But you also know that they consider courses to be a waste of time. So prepare a 'fall-back' position, eg another way of getting them to look at their teaching styles, with your help perhaps.

------------------------------------------------------------✂

# Role play brief

## Appraisee

Your Head of Department is your appraiser.

You tend to be a bit of a 'moaner'.

You have been teaching a long time and use traditional methods in the classroom.

You are not very happy at the school. The children misbehave and you have specific problems with one Year 10 class.

You want to swap teaching this class with the class your HoD has at the same time.

Prepare an approach to achieve this objective.

*Start off the role play by asking if you can make this quick because you are going out tonight.*

# Section Four: Working on the curriculum

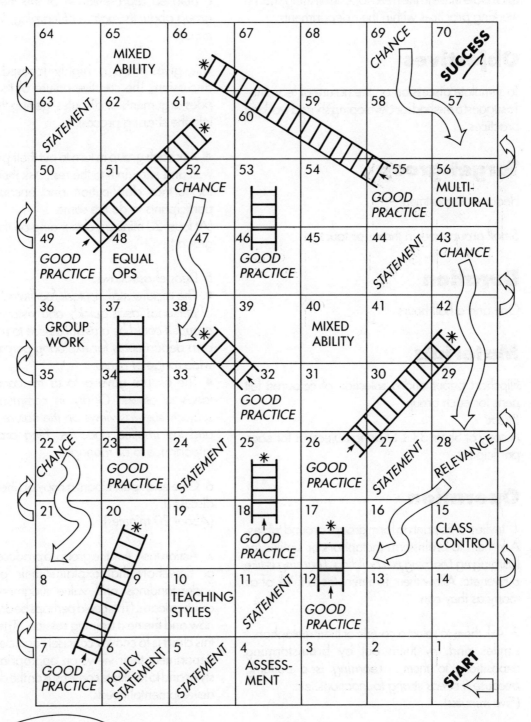

| 64 | 65 MIXED ABILITY | 66 | 67 | 68 | 69 CHANCE | 70 SUCCESS |
|----|----|----|----|----|----|----|
| 63 STATEMENT | 62 | 61 | 60 | 59 | 58 | 57 |
| 50 | 51 | 52 CHANCE | 53 | 54 | 55 GOOD PRACTICE | 56 MULTI-CULTURAL |
| 49 GOOD PRACTICE | 48 EQUAL OPS | 47 | 46 GOOD PRACTICE | 45 | 44 STATEMENT | 43 CHANCE |
| 36 GROUP WORK | 37 | 38 | 39 | 40 MIXED ABILITY | 41 | 42 |
| 35 | 34 | 33 | 32 GOOD PRACTICE | 31 | 30 | 29 |
| 22 CHANCE | 23 GOOD PRACTICE | 24 STATEMENT | 25 | 26 GOOD PRACTICE | 27 STATEMENT | 28 RELEVANCE |
| 21 | 20 | 19 | 18 GOOD PRACTICE | 17 | 16 | 15 CLASS CONTROL |
| 8 | 9 | 10 TEACHING STYLES | 11 STATEMENT | 12 GOOD PRACTICE | 13 | 14 |
| 7 GOOD PRACTICE | 6 POLICY STATEMENT | 5 STATEMENT | 4 ASSESS-MENT | 3 | 2 | 1 START |

WHOSE THROW?

89

# Activity 33 Picture Gallery

This is a simple and adaptable training device which is very useful in facilitating the sharing of perceptions. I use it here to get Heads of Department to assess fundamental criteria for successful learning and relate these to the need for establishing shared working practices within their departments.

## Objectives

To stimulate discussion on the nature of learning
To suggest a method for developing shared working practices

## Target group

Heads of Department

*Small group work* in threes or fours

## Duration

One and a half hours

## Materials

Flipchart paper and a selection of coloured felt pens for each group
*Blutac*
A copy of Sheet 33.1 *Sharing objectives* for each participant

## Operation

1 Invite participants to form groups around tables. Ask them to brainstorm metaphors or similes for learning eg *Learning is a building, Learning is like a river* etc. Allow them five minutes to think of as many as they can.

2 Ask them to select a couple of their metaphors/similes and try them out by brainstorming expositions to them... *Learning is a building because it needs strong foundations.* etc.
(*Five minutes*)

3 Give each group a sheet of flipchart paper and felt pens. Explain as follows:
*Select one of your metaphors/similes and create a picture or diagram of it. The picture should project a detailed representation of the feelings of the group about the nature of learning. You have 20 minutes.*

This gives them a highly focused way-in to discussion. The creative nature of the task over-rides arguments or disputes, getting them straight into the sharing process.

4 Ask each group in turn to put their picture on the wall and explain it to the rest. Ask them questions for further clarification and encourage other participants to do the same.
(*At least 20 minutes, depending on the size of the group.*)

5 Debrief as follows:
• *The picture-making task facilitated the sharing of personal ideas quickly and vividly among the group. It could be a useful device to use with your own departments for exploring perceptions on a wide range of issues.*
• *The picture gave a focus for communicating ideas to others. Clarity in communication (on subjects such as views on the nature of learning and the implied good teaching practice) is of importance to all managers.*

6 Give each participant a copy of Sheet 33.1 and discuss it.
(*About 20 minutes*)

7 *Action task* Ask the group to produce a diagram or flowchart that explains their perceptions, understandings and value judgments on how children learn. (This could perhaps be done between now and the next training session.) The function of this chart is to convey concisely and clearly to their department their views on appropriate teaching styles and to facilitate consensus on the department's developmental needs.

## *In the classroom...*

You'll find the visual representation of ideas very useful in getting children to express their opinions and explore their attitudes. For example: *'Friendship is like a playground!'* ... *draw the playground, illustrate the fun and the problems!*

**Key skills sheet 11**

# Sharing objectives

Part of the job of a Head of Department is to ensure cohesion and consistency within their department, through establishing 'shared objectives'. A structure for facilitating this process is as follows:

1 HoD communicates their own perceptions, understandings and value judgments to their team in an easily-accessible form.

2 The team is asked to contribute their own perceptions, understandings and value judgments. These are compared and contrasted.

3 From 1 and 2 above, a Department Mission Statement is produced.

4 From this Mission Statement, individual and whole-team developmental needs may be assessed and targeted.

Fundamental to the management of a successful curriculum is a shared understanding of how childen learn, so that suitable teaching styles may be adopted for optimum facilitation of this learning.

# Activity 34 Helicopter!

A significant aspect in effective learning is coherence. Subject skills are not used, and concepts not formed, in isolation. So why do we seek to teach them in this way?

It is illuminating to follow a child around for a typical day in a secondary school, covering maybe four or five lessons. The fragmentation is striking. Ask the child in their History lesson at the end of the day what they learned in their Maths lesson at the start of the day and they are unlikely to be able to tell you! The more links we can forge between subjects, the better. Here's an interesting way for you to focus thought upon, and generate activity in, developing cross-curricular links.

## Objectives

To facilitate discussion on the need for cross-curricular links
To explore ways of disseminating information between departments

## Target group

Heads of Department
*Solo and pair work*

## Duration

One and a half hours

## Materials

Flipchart paper for each participant
Felt pens
String – three pieces per pair, measuring two metres, six metres and eight metres respectively
(The school hall or large empty room)

## Operation

1 *Preparation* Ask each participant to bring to the workshop their Scheme of Work or National Curriculum Document for a selected Year Group and time of year: say Year 7, second half of the Autumn term.

2 Give each participant a sheet of flipchart paper and a felt pen. Ask them to write their subject in large capitals at the top of the sheet. Now get them to divide the paper into three columns down the page, headed: Skills, Facts, Concepts (from left to right).

3 Instruct them to refer to their Schemes of Work and enter their learning objectives (for the selected year group and time of year) under the appropriate columns.
(*Allow 20 minutes*)

4 Lay the flipchart sheets out on the floor in a large circle, with the subject headings inwards. Walking around the outside of the circle, you can now read the content of each department's work for this half-term.

5 Ask the participants to form pairs. Give each pair the two and six metre lengths of string. Set the following task:
*Use your pieces of string to join together two subjects where you can see clear links between the skills, facts or concepts stated on the two sheets. Use the short string for a pair that lies close together, the long string for a pair further apart. No cheating with the string lengths!*
(*Allow about ten minutes or so*)

6 Give each pair the eight metre length of string. *Now use this piece to join three subjects together. You are not allowed to start or end on a subject you have previously joined!*
(*Allow another ten minutes*)

7 You will now have a rather dramatic diagram on the floor showing the possible links between subject areas...

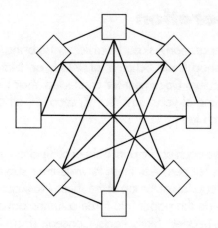

Go into the centre of the circle (carefully!) and choose a few of the stringed-together subjects. Ask the HoDs who placed the string to speak about the links they saw between the subjects.
(*Ten minutes*)

8 Ask partners to discuss the potential usefulness of the 'helicopter vision' this exercise provided. Ask them to focus the discussion on the benefits it might have to a child's learning.
(*Ten minutes*)

9 Get pairs to share their ideas with the rest of the group.
(*20 minutes or so*)

10 Sum-up the benefits of cross-curricular links (providing cohesion, avoiding repetition etc). Discuss as a whole group how information about subject content may be disseminated, so that when potential links are seen they may be exploited.
One way, for example, is to have a 'Year Chart' on the staffroom wall. Each department has a column and very briefly notes the content of their curriculum for the coming half-term.

11 *Action task* Encourage each department to contract a trial link with another department, based on the possibilities they've just observed.

**Key skills sheet 12**

# Activity 35 Centering

The following exercise shows how you can use the 'helicopter' system as a starting point for developing a cross-curricular project.

## Objective

To illustrate how all subject areas may link into a central theme

## Target group

Heads of Department

*Solo work*

## Duration

One and a half hours

## Materials

A toilet roll for each participant
Pens
Flipchart paper
A copy of *Key skills sheet 12* for each participant

## Operation

1 Follow steps 1–4 from Activity 34, so that you achieve a circle of flipchart sheets. Explain the next step:
*Stand on the outside of the circle by your sheet. Now move three sheets in a clockwise direction. Study what is written on the sheet in front of you.*

2 Place another sheet of flipchart paper in the centre, on which you have written, for example 'Myself and the environment'. Give each participant a toilet roll and ask them to join the sheet they are now standing behind to the central one.

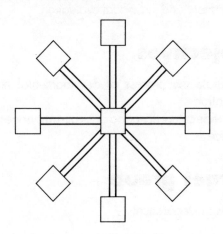

3 Instruct them as follows:
*On the toilet paper, using a felt pen, devise a way the subject objectives may be patched into the central theme of 'Myself and the environment', ie how the content of the former may be learnt in the context of the latter.*

The use of toilet paper adds fun and focus to the activity! Getting participants to work on one another's subjects not only facilitates sharing between departments, it also illustrates how easy it is to link into a theme.

4 Issue participants with a copy of *Key skills sheet 12* – a report on how one school used the above theme across all subjects in Year 7.

# Activity 36 Assessments

Assessing the developmental needs of their team can prove a difficult task for Heads of Department. The exercise below is designed to lay out some criteria for such an assessment and illustrate a process their team might use for whole department and individual evaluation.

## Objectives

To initiate the process of developmental needs evaluation
To provide criteria for good classroom management practice

## Target group

Heads of Department

*Solo work and whole group discussion*

## Duration

About one hour

## Materials

One copy of Sheet 36.1 *Success grid* enlarged to A3 for each participant
One copy of Sheet 36.2 *Good practice pointers* on a sheet of labels for each participant
A second copy of both the above to give out after the session, for their Action Task
Pens

## Operation

1 Give each participant a copy of Sheet 36.1 *Success grid* and explain the task:
*I am going to give you a set of 24 labels. On each label is a pointer to good classroom practice. Remove the labels from the sheet in turn and stick them in the appropriate column on the sheet in front of you; thereby making an assessment of your department.*

2 Give out Sheet 36.2. Allow 20–30 minutes for the task.

3 Debrief...
• *The grid system gives you a way of classifying developmental objectives. You should aim to move all the responses from the three right-hand columns to the left-hand one!*
• *Perhaps the most pressing team developmental needs are the ones in the 'None of Us' or 'Some of Us' columns.*
• *This exercise could be repeated with your department to facilitate consensus of developmental needs. (You could change the headings for the grid, eg 'We are successful at', 'We are less successful at', 'We are unsuccessful at'.) Alternatively, each team member could get a copy for personal assessment, to highlight individual development needs.*

4 Brainstorm other elements of good practice the participants feel have been left out from the labels. Write them up on the flipchart.

5 *Action task* Invite participants to use the assessment device in their departments and from it to produce, say, three developmental targets for the coming year.

## In the classroom...

The stick-in-columns idea is an excellent group work system for the practice of decision-making. It could be used for ranking possible alternatives, eg fragments of a story that the children are asked to assemble, or stages in a scientific experiment that they have to sequence, etc.
    There's something very involving in the physical act of removing the sticker and sticking it on something else; for kids and adults alike!

**Key skills sheets 11 and 12**

# Success grid

| We are all successful at.... | Most of us are successful at.... | Some of us are successful at... | None of us are successful at.... |
|---|---|---|---|
| | | | |

DEPARTMENTAL DEVELOPMENT NEEDS

# Good practice pointers

| | | |
|---|---|---|
| Creating a 'safe' learning environment | Fostering gender equality | Fostering racial equality |
| Communicating relevance | Creating high expectations for *everyone* | Making our subject enjoyable |
| Inculcating self-discipline | Being flexible in our teaching styles | Using a step-by-step approach |
| Facilitating pupils to set themselves individual targets | Teaching self-study skills to the pupils | Motivating |
| Applying a variety of teaching approaches | Questioning old values eg a quiet class x on-task noise √ | Being learning-orientated as opposed to teaching-orientated |
| Building pupils' self-esteem | Building pupils' confidence | Providing challenge |
| Debriefing | Assessing individuals during groupwork | Effective lesson planning |
| Class control | Assessing individuals' learning styles! | Praising |

# Activity 37 The three 'E's

## Objectives

To focus on developmental needs
To explore the 'how' of meeting those needs

## Target group

Heads of Department primarily, but a similar process might be used for Senior Management to look at whole school development needs

*Solo work* followed by small group

## Duration

About one hour

## Materials

A sheet of labels (Sheet 36.2 *Good practice pointers*) for each participant
A sheet of paper and a pen for each participant

## Operation

1 Give each participant a sheet of labels (Sheet 36.2) and a sheet of A4 paper. Ask them to select just one of the labels as a perceived priority for their department. This they stick at the top of the sheet.

2 Invite participants to form groups of four and share the labels they have chosen. Instruct groups as follows:
*Divide your A4 sheet into three sections: 'Entertain', 'Explore' and 'Establish'. Use these headings as a focus for discussing each person's developmental priority, ie*
*a) Entertain – how the HoD can best get their department to 'entertain' the idea that there is a need for this development in their work.*
*b) Explore – how the HoD can get their team members to 'explore' first hand the efficacy of the good classroom management practice*
*c) Establish – how the HoD can best 'establish' the practice as a common one within their department.*

3 *Action task* Ask participants to draw up an action plan for meeting the developmental needs of their department.

# Activity 38 Hierarchies

This is another activity that uses the *Good practice pointers* labels (Sheet 36.2)

## Objective

To explore hierarchies of need in good classroom management practice

## Target group

Heads of Department – to cascade to their teams

*Small groups*

## Operation

1 Ask participants to form small groups. Give each group a sheet of flipchart paper and pens and a copy of the labels sheet (36.2).

2 Ask participants to draw a triangle on the paper and instruct them as follows:
*At the apex of the triangle write 'I am able, I know, I understand' (National Curriculum: Skills, Facts and Concepts). Now use the stickers to fill in the triangle in such a way that perceived fundamentals to successful learning are at the base, and they build hierarchically towards the objective at the apex.*

There are no 'right' answers, but the activity promotes sharing of perceptions and priorities. Later, when the HoDs do this with their own departments, developmental needs may be ranked from the base upwards.

**Key skills sheets 11 and 12**

# Key Skills Sheets

*What do you mean, "I'm too abrasive?"*

# Listening

Effective listening is an active art. It is about communicating willingness to listen, finding and giving time to listen, and asking questions. It is about seeking first to understand rather than to be understood!

- State that you see it as part of your job to listen to the views and problems of others. Reinforce this regularly.
- Try to set aside specific times for listening to people's views and feelings. Let them know when these times are.
- For a variety of reasons we may avoid listening to certain people; ensure that these people also get your ear.
- Avoid, where possible, listening when you haven't really got the time. Instead, make alternative arrangements.

    *Can I come and see you after school for a few moments? I'm really keen on hearing your views but I'm too rushed now.*

- Don't try to listen to someone standing up or across a desk from you. Sit *with* them. If possible go to their home ground (classroom etc).

## *Active* listening

- Be aware of your body language and expression (don't shuffle feet, tap fingers, yawn! etc.)
- Maintain easy eye contact with the person while they are speaking.
- Reinforce the fact you are listening by nodding, by saying 'Yes, I see...' etc.
- Repeat back in paraphrase what the person has just said prior to asking for further explanation. This shows that you really heard what they said!
- Ask questions that 'open the person up'. *Open* questions explore feelings: *Tell me more about how you're getting on with 9-Z... Closed* questions demand simple factual responses: *So you find it hard to control 9-Z?* Open questions may seem quite threatening at first, so progressing from closed to open questions is a useful technique.
- Use your questions to help the other person stay on track. – 'Descriptive, Reflective, Speculative' is a useful sequence here, eg *Can you describe the problem to me? Can you tell me why it's difficult? Can you think of some ways we could get round it?*
- Try to assess the individual's 'sub-textual' needs in speaking to you, so you can address these as well as the verbal content. Ask yourself, *What is this really about? Is this person* (for example) *really just asking for information? Or are they expressing their feelings of not being able to cope?*
- Do not allow outside interruptions to the process.
- Let the other person finish their sentences and line of thought before you say something.

- Don't interrupt them – even (or especially) if you disagree.
- Be aware of your own sensitivities and don't let these get in the way of your listening, eg Don't refuse to listen to things because they make you feel uncomfortable.
- Don't get anecdotal and start talking about yourself! YOU ARE THERE TO LISTEN TO THEM, NOT VICE-VERSA.
- Avoid working out what you are going to say next while you are meant to be listening.
- Observe the other person's body language for signs of discomfort. If you notice such signs, respond to them positively. *It's OK – Take your time and try to tell me how you feel!*
- Listen to *how* things are said as well as *what* is being said. Express this sensitivity, where appropriate,... *I feel you are finding it difficult to speak about this.*
- GIVE PEOPLE SPACE TO EXPRESS THEIR ANGER. ALLOW THEM TO GET UPSET IF THEY NEED TO. It's far too easy to block honest expressions of feelings, or divert people – because they make *us* feel uncomfortable.
- MAKE A POINT OF THANKING PEOPLE AT THE END OF THE CHAT AND EXPRESS HOW USEFUL YOU FOUND IT.

# Negotiating

Good negotiation is about seeking a win/win outcome; where two or more parties agree on a solution or an action that benefits everyone concerned. It's not about trying to get one up. It aims to create allies, not opponents.

## Preparation

1   Have a clear idea of what you want to get out of the negotiation:
●   an ideal outcome
●   a compromise scenario
●   an acceptable minimum outcome.
2   Define no more than two or three strong arguments to support your case.
3   Know the weaknesses of your arguments and prepare to compensate for them.
4   Support your case with evidence of need specific to your organisation and/or the other party.
5   Assess the other side's likely responses:
●   prepare to counter likely points of resistance;
●   prepare your approach proactively to counter negative feelings.
6   Assess the other side's strengths and play to them.
7   Ask for more than what you want!
8   Set realistic timescales for developments.
9   Solicit allies if appropriate.
10  Mentally rehearse the negotiation and your approach to it.
11  Having well-thought-out proposals written up (with a copy for the other party) might be useful during the negotiation. Consider whether or not it would be productive to give them this prior to your meeting.

## Basic strategies during negotiation

1   Focus on establishing a rapport with the other party first.
2   Focus on *active listening* as opposed to talking.
3   Don't, if possible, state your case first:
●   use questioning to seek to understand their position and ideally lead them into stating your case for you.
4   Seek to engage the other side positively in the negotiating process. Try approaches like, *I am interested in hearing your views on X* and *I should like your advice on how we could best proceed in X.* These are far more likely to produce results than *I want to do this...*
5   Show sensitivity to the problems they have and state these understandings: *I realise you have a lot on your plate at the moment.*
6   Seek to establish common ground first.

7    Anticipate positive responses in the way you phrase your statements, but don't presume – it's better to say *I feel you would agree with me when I say X* rather than *I am sure you would agree with me when I say X.*

8    State your case in terms that suit *their* frame of reference and level of understanding.

9    Clearly explain the 'Whys' behind your arguments.

## Handling negative responses

1    Don't state your disagreements. Rather, get the other party to question the validity of their own views: *That's interesting. How would it work if...* etc.

2    Don't tell the other party *Why* their argument is wrong, use the above process to *lead* them into this discovery.

3    Affirm the validity of their opinions in a way that develops consensus: *Yes, that's an important point. How do you think we could overcome that problem?*

4    Be concessional wherever possible, but make concessions conditional: *If we don't do X then perhaps we could do Y.*

5    Avoid phrases that put the other party down in any way, eg *With respect..That's typical!* etc.

6    Use 'However' instead of 'But'.

7    Use 'I feel' rather than 'I think'.

8    Don't allow yourself to lose your calm or be hectored by time elements; arrange another meeting rather than rushing this one.

9    Should all other strategies seem to be failing, state calmly and assertively how you feel about their intransigence.

10   If you feel they are being insensitive to you, then tell them so calmly: *I feel you are not crediting me with having thought this through.*

11   Only make threats as a last resort and then only if you have the authority and intention to carry them out.

12   When you see an error in your own thinking or behaviour, admit it!

13   If agreement cannot be reached, buy time for further consideration.

## Summarising

1    Recap on what has been agreed. If appropriate, reinforce this by written memo later.

2    Recap on any 'sticking points' that might be referred back to at a later date.

3    Recap on time scales and deadlines for action to be taken.

4    State your understandings of any help the other party has contracted to you.

5    Set times for further consultation and evaluation.

6    State your appreciation of the positive way in which the other party has conducted themselves.

# Delegation

Where feasible, a Manager should delegate everything that is not their direct responsibility and that is not of direct importance to their role, function or mission. When anything lands on your desk, ask the question *Why me?* If a subordinate is able to do it effectively, they should *be* doing it.

## Lines of delegation

There are three lines of delegation:

1  UPWARDS
- This is not within my remit or role definition and is important.
- This is something that I need support/guidance on
- This is something my boss(es) needs to know about.
- This is something I could handle but my boss has a specific brief for it/interest in it/ wants to be kept informed about it.

2  SIDEWAYS
- This is not within my remit or role defintion and/or someone at my own line management level is better equipped to deal with it.
- Someone at my own line management level has a specific brief/interest that this falls under.
- This is something we need to work on at line management level as a team.

3  DOWNWARDS
- This is not worth my time but is worth someone else's time for reasons of staff development/interest.
- Someone else should do this for logistical reasons, so that we share chores.
- Sharing this task with the team is good for team-building.

## Ground rules for downward delegation...

1  Do not dump. If you do (!) ensure that you dump fairly, equally and explain your reasons: *I haven't got time, I'd be grateful if you'd do this for us.*

2  You can delegate both tasks and roles. The more precisely you pre-define roles the easier it is to delegate to them.

3  Delegate to the *lowest suitable level* of responsibility since it is good for developing initiative and involvement.

4  Once something significant is delegated, leave it to them to do it. Don't tell them *how* to do it. Support and review progress, ask to be kept informed, but let them take the initiative for managing the task themself.

5  Never take back what has been delegated. Support and facilitate more if necessary. Taking back an important task is bad for morale and staff development.

106                                    © Geoff Hannan/Simon & Schuster Ltd 1992

# In practice...

Devise a written system for yourself, eg a sheet of paper divided into headings such as *Urgent and Important; Important but Not Urgent; Urgent but Not Important; Not Important and Not Urgent.* Each heading could be further sub-divided with the names of your team. When a task comes in, define it under the heading.

Remember...*Important but Not Urgent* is your column!

Teach the art of delegation to your team as well.

# Assertiveness

Assertiveness is not about domination or about getting your own way. It is about being clear, open and honest in your dealings with other people. To be assertive requires you to be calm and considered in any situation. It is an art that needs practice and planning until we become skilled in it.

## In harmony

• Find time to express your feelings of satisfaction with other people. Make the expression personal:....*Thank you for letting me see your lesson. You really taught it well.* (NOT *It was a good lesson.*)

• Express how the other person made *you* feel. *Thank you for arranging the show for parents' evening. I felt really proud of what you achieved with other pupils.*

• Find ways of ensuring that the other person trusts your compliments and does not view them as being manipulative. When you want something from them is *not* the time to compliment someone.

• Be as specific as possible in your compliments:... *You really handled that situation with Jimmy Smith well. He was fuming and you calmed him down wonderfully by the quiet way you spoke to him!*

• Do not shrug-off other people's compliments to you, learn to accept them totally. *Thank you, I appreciate you telling me that! I find it reassuring that you think this way too!*

## In discord

• Plan and mentally rehearse what you are going to say and how and when you are going to say it.

• Use the word 'feel' as opposed to 'think'.... *I feel your work is deteriorating.*

• Be sensitive to the other person's problems and show this sensitivity: *I feel your work is deteriorating, have you got problems I can help you with?*

• Ensure that the other person knows it is their behaviour you have problems with and not them personally, by separating them from their mistake: *I feel angry that the report you promised me isn't in yet. You're an important member of this team whose views I really value!*

• Express openly how the other person's behaviour affects you: *When you speak to me like that in front of others in the staffroom, it embarrasses me.*

• Try to be as specific as possible, and avoid general labelling, ie NOT *You are insensitive* BUT *At times during staff meetings you tend to be insensitive to the feelings of others.*

# Leadership

There are three key components to leadership: team building; development of individuals; managing yourself.

## 1  Build the team to achieve the task

● Concentrate on *motivation* – remember that different people are encouraged and motivated by different things ('Different Strokes for Different Folks').
● Be sure to thank people. Some people need praise in private, others publicly.
● Ask for opinions and wherever possible consult before reaching important decisions.
● Praise good work and initiative.
● Be honest and open in your dealings with the team and demand the same from them.
● Challenge.
● Negotiate and clearly define roles within the team whilst encouraging cross-fertilisation and role exchange.
● Negotiate and clearly define 'mission'.
● Negotiate and clearly define aims *and* objectives.
● Set achievable targets with deadlines.
● Build a team culture: *This is how we do things here.*
● Negotiate and clearly define criteria for success.
● Set up a system for evaluating and appraising team performance.
● Ensure that working conditions are good.
● Ensure that resources are adequate.
● Encourage team members to join unions.
● Deal with gripes and grievances quickly.
● Manage by wandering around...observe, listen, praise.
● Assess the whole team's developmental needs and provide training.

## 2  Develop individuals

● Assess each individual's developmental needs and provide training.
● Negotiate and set individual targets for development.
● Be directive to the inexperienced, consultatory especially with the experienced.
● Be supportive to everyone, but not over-supportive as this may discourage autonomous action and initiative.
● Openly invite people to share their problems with you.
● Delegate as much as possible, and equitably.
● Ensure that each individual knows their function in the team and has specific responsibilities.

- Install a system for positive appraisal of each individual's performance.
- Understand each individual's particular motivation.
- Get them to work through their strengths.
- Reprimand promptly and sensitively when required, always separating the person from the mistake.
- Encourage innovation.
- Encourage individual interests.
- Become holistic in your approach to everyone... manage the person first, the professional next.
- Praise!

## 3  Managing yourself

- Lead by actions, not words.
- Don't say one thing and do another.
- Manage your time efficiently.
- Make sure you give yourself time to listen to people.
- See yourself as a counsellor as well as a boss.
- See yourself achieving results *through others*.
- Be sensitive to your own needs and communicate them.
- Work on your strengths and develop others to compensate for your weaknesses.
- Never allow yourself to become aggressive.
- Define and communicate your perceptions of your role.
- Define the things about which you and you alone make decisions and communicate them.
- Define your 'needs to know' and communicate them.
- Admit mistakes and give yourself credit!

# Teamwork

Effective teamwork is the working together of like-minded individuals towards shared objectives. It is about knowing *who* is going, *where* you are going, and *how* all of you are going to get there!

- Know the individual strengths within your team and utilise these strengths to the full.
- Know the weaknesses of the team as a whole and organise training to compensate.
- Seek to develop a team 'culture' and 'identity': *We work in such-and-such a way...*
- Closely define functions within the team and ensure each person understands their own role and function(s).
- Where possible, delegate decision-making as well as action to individuals within the team.
- Know and use the resources of the 'invisible teams'... the other teams your individual team members belong to.
- Separate tasks effectively and without duplication.
- Discuss and consult at regular intervals. Remember the '4 Ps':
  1 How the *people* in the team are working together, what problems they have, etc.
  2 and 3 *Policy* and *progress* – reviewing how the team is progressing towards its shared objectives.
  4 *Points* – the pressing and specific issues that need to be addressed now to keep everyone happy and on course.
- Monitor action effectively to learn from successes and failures.
- Spend as much time together as possible!

# The management of change

Change is a garden. It is made up of individual plants tended separately towards a vision of the whole.

## Planning

- Define your vision of the organisation after the change.
- Write out simply and concisely the benefits of the change.
- Work backwards – plan for the long-term but target for the short-term. Set short-term goals in 'real' timescales.
- Assess likely negative effects and plan steps to counter them.
- Define areas of least resistance (people likely to be in favour of the change straight away etc). Plan to involve them from the outset.
- Plan to involve important people on the 'periphery' of the organisation/Governors etc.
- Set our your criteria for success from the outset.
- Set out a method for evaluating how the development is progressing.
- Set a realistic timescale.

## Implementation

- Initiate the change process from the top but *also* manage it from the bottom to develop ownership.
- Consider a staff consultatory process early on.
- Select members of staff and delegate specific responsibilities to them.
- Consider delegating the overall responsibility of the change management to one member of staff under your guidance.
- Consider introducing the change in the most receptive areas of the organisation first, perhaps on a trial basis.
- Solicit feedback from the outset.
- Deal with any problems encountered immediately as they occur.
- Don't expend too much of your energies on disapproving minorities! Give them your support and encouragement but move the majority forward.
- Give carrots and let people know what's in it for them!
- Set deadlines and stick to them.
- Consider setting up a working party led by *someone else* that you trust. This is an excellent way of developing 'ownership'.

# Action planning

## Section One: Developmental Objective

Define the objective precisely and concisely...

To _____

For what reason _____

Target date/by _____

## Section Two: Pro-Active Planning

(i) Define the likely
difficulties involved

(ii) Define ways of overcoming
these difficulties

Probable problems in
achieving development:                    Countered by

1 _____
2 _____
3 _____
4 _____
5 _____

## Section Three: Task Definitions

A *Define appropriate tasks to achieve the development. A number of these should be carefully devised pro-active measures to counter the probable problems defined in Section Two.*

Deadlines

1 _____
2 _____
3 _____
4 _____
5 _____

B Others *Define bureaucratic and logistical tasks needed...*

_____
_____
_____

*Ascribe deadlines to each of the above*

## Section Four: Task Separation

From the tasks in Section Three, consult with your team and delegate specific responsibilities to individuals....

Name_____

To _____

For (Statement of purpose): _____

How _____

By_____

Criteria for success _____

– – – – – – – – – – – – – – – – – – – – – – – – – – – – – – –

Name_____

To _____

For (Statement of purpose): _____

How _____

By_____

Criteria for success _____

– – – – – – – – – – – – – – – – – – – – – – – – – – – – – – –

Name_____

To _____

For (Statement of purpose): _____

How _____

By_____

Criteria for success _____

– – – – – – – – – – – – – – – – – – – – – – – – – – – – – – –

## Section Five: Time Scaling

Week 1 2 3 4 5 6 7 8 9 10 11 12 (etc).

Meeting one

To _____

Meeting two

To _____

Evaluation process _____

# Meetings

The best meetings are 'managed' meetings...

SCENARIO   You are meeting an outsider to your organisation. The meeting takes place in your own office. (Much of the following is equally applicable to other one-to-one meetings.)

## Preparation

**1   Territory**

Position both chairs equally in the meeting room.
Provide some neutral space between the chairs, eg a coffee table, a round table, the corner of a rectangular table. DON'T sit behind your desk, or face-to-face.

**2   Time**

Ensure you allow long enough for the meeting.
Let others know you are not to be disturbed. DON'T allow interruptions.

**3   Materials**

Have pens and paper for their use as well as your own.
Have anything you may wish to give them ready to hand. Give it in a folder with their name and your letterhead on it.
Have the coffee ready.

**4   Mental**

Define your objectives.
Sequence the points to be covered.

## Greetings

1   Be ready to come straight down to meet them at reception.
DON'T have them brought/shown to you.
2   Smile and shake hands.
3   Thank them for coming.
4   Seek first to establish a rapport with the person, not the 'professional':
   - thank them for their punctuality
   - enquire into their ease of getting to you
   - as you take them to your office, explain the work areas you are moving through
   - express sensitivity to their needs, eg 'The toilets are...'

- ask them about themselves...

DON'T talk about yourself first. DON'T moan about how busy you are.

5 Keep easy, eye-to-eye contact. DON'T stare.

6 Offer them refreshment. DON'T leave them alone to make it yourself.

## Openings

1 Ask and indicate for them to sit.

2 Mirror their sitting position as you sit next to them.

DON'T present barrier body language – folded arms, etc.

3 State your objectives for the meeting.

4 Enquire into their additional objectives: 'Is there anything else you feel it would be useful for us to discuss?' DON'T fail to take the initial lead.

5 State or show the importance you give to meeting them. For example, use your intercom/phone to restate your desire not to be disturbed.

6 Use negotiating language – 'Perhaps we could start by...'.

7 Sequence discussion
- ask them questions
- show you are listening by initially restating what they say prior to asking for further clarification or information: 'So you think this, this, and this... how about this?'
- show you are listening by nodding

DON'T look at papers, out of the window, at your watch... while they are talking
- Sequence: descriptive... reflective... speculative

'Perhaps you could tell me a little about your work?'

'Perhaps we could reflect upon how we could help one-another?'

'Let's think about practical outcomes.'

## During

1 Take notes – and make sure they can see what you are writing

2 Reinforce that their interests are at least as important as your own.

AVOID being too anecdotal.

## Concluding

1 Sum up content and conclusions.

2 Express how useful the meeting has been.

3 Check you have one-another's phone numbers.

4 Show them all the way out.

5 Thank them for coming.

6 Shake hands again.

7 Write a follow-up letter outlining conclusions and thanking them again.

# Appraisal

The following notes are designed to trigger thinking on strategies for a positive appraisal process for your school.

## Purposes of appraisal

- To provide on-going support to members of your team.
- To assist individual members of your team in their professional development.
- To *mutually* assess and *negotiate* individual developmental targets.
- To obtain constructive comment on your effectiveness as a manager.
- To translate the above into positive outcomes for the individual, yourself, the team and the organisation.
- To create an atmosphere of mutual support.

## The appraisal interview

- The interview should be part of a regular process to help achieve the above aims.
- A precursor to it should be a process of self-appraisal.
- The self-appraisal might be formulated along lines mutually negotiated by the manager and their team.

## Structure for an appraisal interview

| PLAN | | OBJECTIVES |
|---|---|---|
| | STEP ONE | |
| Establish rapport | | Keeping intial interaction friendly, relaxed and businesslike |
| Getting to know how they feel about the appraisal process | | Allay fears |
| | STEP TWO | |
| Sharing interview objectives with appraisee | | Agree mutual objectives |
| Exploring their interview objectives | | Establish atmosphere of trust and co-operation |
| | STEP THREE | |
| Itemising and raising specific issues to be discussed | | Dealing with issues methodically and sequentially |
| | STEP FOUR | |
| In dealing with issues, expressing areas of agreement and disagreement | | Reaching consensus |
| | STEP FIVE | |
| Evaluation of agreements reached Goal setting and targetting Contracting support | | Agreeing what has been agreed! |
| | STEP SIX | |
| Affirmation of agreement | | Putting agreement in writing |

# Classroom observations

Observation is 'purposeful looking'! The list below suggests things to look for with the purpose of benefiting both teacher and pupils...

## Timings

- Was time managed well during the lesson?
- Introduction the right length?
- Activities the right length?
- Enough time allowed for debrief?

## Structure

- Planned well?
- Objectives defined and achieved?
- Pitched at the right level?
- Enough challenge?
- Enough variety?
- Flexible enough?

## Materials

- Interesting enough?
- Relevant?
- Multicultural/gender friendly?

## Teaching styles

- Appropriate to content/pupil understanding?
- Pupil-centred?
- Varied enough?
- Was relevance communicated?
- A step-by-step approach?
- Confidence/esteem building?
- Motivation given?
- Expectations high?
- Pupil involvement generated/ownership developed?
- Pupils felt successful?
- Lesson enjoyable?

## Classroom management

- Instructions clearly given?
- Well ordered?
- Pupils 'on task'?
- Opportunities given for pupil/pupil discussion?
- Behavioural conventions understood/followed?
- Disruption handled well?
- Problems minimised?
- Enough praise given?
- Equal teacher time devoted to girls and boys?
- Equal contributions from girls and boys?
- Use of solo, pair and group work?
- Effectiveness of groupings (extroverts together, introverts together etc)?
- Opportunities for one-to-one contact?
- Questioning strategies effective?

# Cross-curricular projects

*With thanks to the Head and Staff of Springhill High School – Rochdale, here are some things to bear in mind and some ideas to help you get started on cross-curricular projects...*

## Useful prerequisites

- A HoD and departmental meeting structure under Head-directed time.
- A timetabling structure where pupils are 'subject blocked' in, for example, half-year groupings.
- An active learning/pupil-centred approach to teaching!
- A clear understanding of why cross-curricular links enhance pupil learning (by adding planned coherence and cohesion to the learning experience, reinforcing relevance, creating a memorable programme etc).
- Teachers committed to the challenge of working creatively together.
- A teacher in each department responsible for cross-curricular links/HoDs with such a responsibility in their job description.
- Financial resources (albeit limited), centrally appropriated.
- The goodwill of staff!

## Pointers

*Don't be put off by the seeming complexity: you, the pupils and the project itself will find a way through it to good advantage.*

1    Select a theme that is broad enough but not too broad. Ideas: 'The School and its community' 'Patterns' 'Structures' 'Life Styles' 'Time' 'Myself, others and the environment' 'Animals and their Welfare' 'One World'.

2    All departments must be involved and the theme must respect individual specialisms. If a department says, *This theme is no good for us!'* extend/adapt the theme! eg 'Healthy Living' could be extended by curriculum needs of History into 'Life Styles'. Avoid 'token' involvement!

3    Set a date for the project start and decide on its duration well in advance. Allow for flexibility by setting a minimum period: two weeks, for example, but some departments may wish to *over*-run.

4    Get all HoDs or cross-curriculum reps together for an initial planning meeting, then give them time to go back to their departments for consultation and further planning.

5    Distrubute a pro forma to each Department that asks them to explain their contribution in some detail with the projected number of lessons they feel they'll need to complete the project. On this ask them to note potential links with other departments.

6    Collate the above. Identify overlap and eliminate by negotiation.

7    Identify the possibilities for Departments to work together.